**TEACHER'S PET PUBLICATIONS**

PUZZLE PACK
for
Fever 1793

based on the book by
Laurie Halse Anderson

Written by
Mary B. Collins

© 2007 Teacher's Pet Publications
All Rights Reserved

The materials in this packet are copyrighted
by Teacher's Pet Publications, Inc.

These pages may be duplicated by the purchaser
for use in the purchaser's own classroom.

Copying any of these materials and distributing them
for any other purpose is a violation of the copyright laws.

© 2007 Teacher's Pet Publications, Inc.
www.tpet.com

INTRODUCTION
If you already own the LitPlan for this title, this Puzzle Pack will refresh your Unit Resource Materials and Vocabulary Resource Materials sections plus give you additional materials you can substitute into the tests. If you do not already have a complete LitPlan, these pages will give you some supplemental materials to use with your own plan. There are two main groups of materials: one set for unit words (such as characters' names, symbols, places, etc.) and one set for vocabulary words associated with the book.

WORD LIST
There is a word list for both the unit words and the vocabulary words. These lists show you which words are being used in the materials and the clues or definitions being used for those words. You may want to give students a word list with clues/definitions to help them, or you may want students to only have a word list (without clues/definitions) if you want them to work a little harder. Both are available for duplication. The word lists can also be your "calling key" for the bingo games.

FILL IN THE BLANK AND MATCHING
There are 4 each of the fill in the blank and matching worksheets for both the unit and vocabulary words. These pages can be used either as extra worksheets for students or as objective parts of a unit test. They can be done individually if students need extra help or as a whole class activity to review the material covered.

MAGIC SQUARES
The magic squares not only reinforce the material covered but also work on reasoning and math skills. Many teachers have told us that their students really enjoy doing these!

WORD SEARCH PUZZLES
The word search words go in all directions, as indicated on your answer keys. Two of the word search puzzles have the clues listed rather than the words. This makes the puzzle a little more difficult, but it reinforces the material better. Two word search puzzles have words only for students who find the clue puzzles too difficult.

CROSSWORD PUZZLES
Both unit and vocabulary word sections have 4 crossword puzzles.

BINGO CARDS
There are 32 individual bingo cards for the unit words and 32 individual bingo cards for the vocabulary words. You can use your word list as a "call list," calling the words at random and marking them off of your list as you go, or you could use the flash cards by cutting them apart and drawing the words at random from a hat (or box or whatever). To make a better review, you might ask for the definition and spelling of each word as you call it out–or you could call out the definitions and have students tell you the words they need to look for on the puzzle.

JUGGLE LETTERS
The vocabulary juggle letter game is intended to help students learn the spellings of the words. One sheet has the definitions listed on it as an extra help for students who need it or to reinforce the definitions if you choose to do so.

FLASH CARDS
We've included a set of vocabulary flash cards you can duplicate, cut, and fold for your students. Some teachers make a few sets for general use by the class; others make a set for each student. Some teachers duplicate them for each student and have the students cut & fold their own. You can cut out just the words and put them in a hat, have each student pick out one word and write the definition and a sentence for that word. Students then swap words and papers, with the next student adding a sentence of his own under the last one. You can have students swap as many times as you like. Each time the student will read the sentences written prior to his own and then add a sentence. You can cut out the words and definitions separately and play "I Have; Who Has?" Each student in the room draws a word and definition. The first student says, "I have (the name of the word). Who has the definition?" The student with the definition reads it then says, "I have (the name of the vocabulary word she has). Who has the definition?" The round continues until all words and definitions have been given.

Fever 1793 Word List

No.	Word	Clue/Definition
1.	ANDERSON	Author
2.	BATHE	Matilda does this once a month and on special occasions.
3.	BELLS	These ring whenever someone dies.
4.	BIBLE	Matilda likes to read it at the end of each day.
5.	BUSH	Matilda is taken to ___ Hill to recover from yellow fever.
6.	CART	A man dumps Matilda's mother off of one.
7.	CHURN	Chore to keep the children busy: ___ butter
8.	COLETTE	Eloped with her French tutor
9.	COUNTRY	Wealthy people flee there to escape the fever.
10.	DOWRY	Joseph thinks Matilda should sell the coffeehouse so she has a nice ___.
11.	ELIZA	Coffeehouse partner with Matilda
12.	FATHER	He fell off a ladder and died of a broken neck.
13.	FLAGG	Grandfather flirts with her as she nurses Matilda back to health.
14.	FLOWERS	Nathaniel Benson throws these out a window at Matilda and Eliza.
15.	FRANCE	Country Matilda wants to go to
16.	FRENCH	These doctors know how to treat the fever better than anyone else.
17.	FROST	It kills off the mosquitoes and the yellow fever.
18.	GARDEN	Place Matilda's grandfather wants her to get their food
19.	GEORGE	Parrot's name: King ___
20.	GIRARD	Stephen ___ turns Bush Hill into a safe hospital.
21.	JEFFERSON	Matilda wants to get Thomas ___ to eat at the coffeehouse.
22.	JOSEPH	Eliza's brother who lost his wife to yellow fever
23.	LUDINGTON	Family whose farm Matilda's mother wants to send her to
24.	MARKET	Place where people buy and sell food
25.	MOTHER	She is assumed dead but comes back to the coffeehouse at the end.
26.	NELL	Small child Matilda finds and cares for
27.	OGLIVIE	Family Matilda's mother hopes her daughter can marry into
28.	ORPHANAGE	Place the people at Bush Hill want Matilda to go to help out
29.	PAINTER	Nathaniel Benson's job
30.	PEALE	Nathaniel sends Matilda a note saying he is safe at ___'s house.
31.	PEARS	Matilda is gathering these when she passes out, sick with the fever
32.	POLLY	Girl who worked at the coffeehouse who dies of yellow fever
33.	PORTRAIT	Item Matilda buries with her grandfather
34.	PRAYER	Matilda has to fight to get one said at her grandfather's funeral.
35.	REFUGEES	People Matilda's grandfather thinks are to blame for the fever
36.	ROBBED	Matilda and her grandfather return to Philadelphia & discover they were ___.
37.	RUSH	He believes black people can't catch yellow fever.
38.	SAWDUST	People mixed it with flour to make more bread.
39.	SILAS	The cat's name
40.	SKIRT	Matilda uses this to try to catch fish.
41.	STRONGBOX	Hiding place for coffeehouse money
42.	SWORD	Matilda stabs the robber with it.
43.	WAGON	Transportation to the country
44.	WALK	What Matilda and Nathaniel do every evening
45.	WASHINGTON	Business grows when George ___ builds a home a few blocks away.
46.	WHARVES	Matilda's mother forbids her to go there for fear she might get sick.
47.	WILLOW	Matilda searches for this kind of a tree, knowing water will be nearby.

Fever 1793 Fill In The Blanks 1

_____

_____

_____

_____

_____

_____

_____

_____

_____

_____

_____

_____

_____

_____

_____

_____

_____

_____

_____

_____

1. Parrot's name: King ___
2. Matilda has to fight to get one said at her grandfather's funeral.
3. Country Matilda wants to go to
4. Girl who worked at the coffeehouse who dies of yellow fever
5. What Matilda and Nathaniel do every evening
6. Matilda uses this to try to catch fish.
7. Matilda wants to get Thomas ___ to eat at the coffeehouse.
8. Matilda does this once a month and on special occasions.
9. She is assumed dead but comes back to the coffeehouse at the end.
10. Matilda searches for this kind of a tree, knowing water will be nearby.
11. Nathaniel sends Matilda a note saying he is safe at ___'s house.
12. Matilda and her grandfather return to Philadelphia & discover they were ___.
13. Place where people buy and sell food
14. Joseph thinks Matilda should sell the coffeehouse so she has a nice ___.
15. Eliza's brother who lost his wife to yellow fever
16. People mixed it with flour to make more bread.
17. It kills off the mosquitoes and the yellow fever.
18. People Matilda's grandfather thinks are to blame for the fever
19. Matilda is gathering these when she passes out, sick with the fever
20. Chore to keep the children busy: ___ butter

Fever 1793 Fill In The Blanks 1 Answer Key

GEORGE	1. Parrot's name: King ___
PRAYER	2. Matilda has to fight to get one said at her grandfather's funeral.
FRANCE	3. Country Matilda wants to go to
POLLY	4. Girl who worked at the coffeehouse who dies of yellow fever
WALK	5. What Matilda and Nathaniel do every evening
SKIRT	6. Matilda uses this to try to catch fish.
JEFFERSON	7. Matilda wants to get Thomas ___ to eat at the coffeehouse.
BATHE	8. Matilda does this once a month and on special occasions.
MOTHER	9. She is assumed dead but comes back to the coffeehouse at the end.
WILLOW	10. Matilda searches for this kind of a tree, knowing water will be nearby.
PEALE	11. Nathaniel sends Matilda a note saying he is safe at ___'s house.
ROBBED	12. Matilda and her grandfather return to Philadelphia & discover they were ___.
MARKET	13. Place where people buy and sell food
DOWRY	14. Joseph thinks Matilda should sell the coffeehouse so she has a nice ___.
JOSEPH	15. Eliza's brother who lost his wife to yellow fever
SAWDUST	16. People mixed it with flour to make more bread.
FROST	17. It kills off the mosquitoes and the yellow fever.
REFUGEES	18. People Matilda's grandfather thinks are to blame for the fever
PEARS	19. Matilda is gathering these when she passes out, sick with the fever
CHURN	20. Chore to keep the children busy: ___ butter

Fever 1793 Fill In The Blanks 2

_____

_____

_____

_____

_____

_____

_____

_____

_____

_____

_____

_____

_____

_____

_____

_____

_____

_____

_____

_____

1. People Matilda's grandfather thinks are to blame for the fever
2. Nathaniel Benson's job
3. Matilda's mother forbids her to go there for fear she might get sick.
4. Matilda is gathering these when she passes out, sick with the fever
5. Matilda searches for this kind of a tree, knowing water will be nearby.
6. Family Matilda's mother hopes her daughter can marry into
7. Eliza's brother who lost his wife to yellow fever
8. Matilda wants to get Thomas ___ to eat at the coffeehouse.
9. Nathaniel sends Matilda a note saying he is safe at ___'s house.
10. Matilda likes to read it at the end of each day.
11. Matilda uses this to try to catch fish.
12. He fell off a ladder and died of a broken neck.
13. Joseph thinks Matilda should sell the coffeehouse so she has a nice ___.
14. Place where people buy and sell food
15. Country Matilda wants to go to
16. Girl who worked at the coffeehouse who dies of yellow fever
17. Place the people at Bush Hill want Matilda to go to help out
18. Business grows when George ___ builds a home a few blocks away.
19. Matilda and her grandfather return to Philadelphia & discover they were ___.
20. Place Matilda's grandfather wants her to get their food

Fever 1793 Fill In The Blanks 2 Answer Key

REFUGEES	1.	People Matilda's grandfather thinks are to blame for the fever
PAINTER	2.	Nathaniel Benson's job
WHARVES	3.	Matilda's mother forbids her to go there for fear she might get sick.
PEARS	4.	Matilda is gathering these when she passes out, sick with the fever
WILLOW	5.	Matilda searches for this kind of a tree, knowing water will be nearby.
OGLIVIE	6.	Family Matilda's mother hopes her daughter can marry into
JOSEPH	7.	Eliza's brother who lost his wife to yellow fever
JEFFERSON	8.	Matilda wants to get Thomas ___ to eat at the coffeehouse.
PEALE	9.	Nathaniel sends Matilda a note saying he is safe at ___'s house.
BIBLE	10.	Matilda likes to read it at the end of each day.
SKIRT	11.	Matilda uses this to try to catch fish.
FATHER	12.	He fell off a ladder and died of a broken neck.
DOWRY	13.	Joseph thinks Matilda should sell the coffeehouse so she has a nice ___.
MARKET	14.	Place where people buy and sell food
FRANCE	15.	Country Matilda wants to go to
POLLY	16.	Girl who worked at the coffeehouse who dies of yellow fever
ORPHANAGE	17.	Place the people at Bush Hill want Matilda to go to help out
WASHINGTON	18.	Business grows when George ___ builds a home a few blocks away.
ROBBED	19.	Matilda and her grandfather return to Philadelphia & discover they were ___.
GARDEN	20.	Place Matilda's grandfather wants her to get their food

Fever 1793 Fill In The Blanks 3

_____

_____

_____

_____

_____

_____

_____

_____

_____

_____

_____

_____

_____

_____

_____

_____

_____

_____

_____

_____

1. Matilda stabs the robber with it.
2. Grandfather flirts with her as she nurses Matilda back to health.
3. He believes black people can't catch yellow fever.
4. People mixed it with flour to make more bread.
5. Stephen ___ turns Bush Hill into a safe hospital.
6. Nathaniel sends Matilda a note saying he is safe at ___'s house.
7. Author
8. Matilda and her grandfather return to Philadelphia & discover they were ___.
9. Family whose farm Matilda's mother wants to send her to
10. Matilda is gathering these when she passes out, sick with the fever
11. These doctors know how to treat the fever better than anyone else.
12. Matilda does this once a month and on special occasions.
13. Place the people at Bush Hill want Matilda to go to help out
14. Item Matilda buries with her grandfather
15. Parrot's name: King ___
16. What Matilda and Nathaniel do every evening
17. He fell off a ladder and died of a broken neck.
18. Eloped with her French tutor
19. Wealthy people flee there to escape the fever.
20. It kills off the mosquitoes and the yellow fever.

Fever 1793 Fill In The Blanks 3 Answer Key

SWORD	1.	Matilda stabs the robber with it.
FLAGG	2.	Grandfather flirts with her as she nurses Matilda back to health.
RUSH	3.	He believes black people can't catch yellow fever.
SAWDUST	4.	People mixed it with flour to make more bread.
GIRARD	5.	Stephen ___ turns Bush Hill into a safe hospital.
PEALE	6.	Nathaniel sends Matilda a note saying he is safe at ___'s house.
ANDERSON	7.	Author
ROBBED	8.	Matilda and her grandfather return to Philadelphia & discover they were ___.
LUDINGTON	9.	Family whose farm Matilda's mother wants to send her to
PEARS	10.	Matilda is gathering these when she passes out, sick with the fever
FRENCH	11.	These doctors know how to treat the fever better than anyone else.
BATHE	12.	Matilda does this once a month and on special occasions.
ORPHANAGE	13.	Place the people at Bush Hill want Matilda to go to help out
PORTRAIT	14.	Item Matilda buries with her grandfather
GEORGE	15.	Parrot's name: King ___
WALK	16.	What Matilda and Nathaniel do every evening
FATHER	17.	He fell off a ladder and died of a broken neck.
COLETTE	18.	Eloped with her French tutor
COUNTRY	19.	Wealthy people flee there to escape the fever.
FROST	20.	It kills off the mosquitoes and the yellow fever.

Fever 1793 Fill In The Blanks 4

_____

_____

_____

_____

_____

_____

_____

_____

_____

_____

_____

_____

_____

_____

_____

_____

_____

_____

_____

_____

1. These ring whenever someone dies.
2. Matilda does this once a month and on special occasions.
3. A man dumps Matilda's mother off of one.
4. Matilda stabs the robber with it.
5. She is assumed dead but comes back to the coffeehouse at the end.
6. Business grows when George ___ builds a home a few blocks away.
7. Matilda uses this to try to catch fish.
8. Matilda likes to read it at the end of each day.
9. The cat's name
10. Transportation to the country
11. Wealthy people flee there to escape the fever.
12. Matilda and her grandfather return to Philadelphia & discover they were ___.
13. Parrot's name: King ___
14. Family Matilda's mother hopes her daughter can marry into
15. Place Matilda's grandfather wants her to get their food
16. It kills off the mosquitoes and the yellow fever.
17. Matilda wants to get Thomas ___ to eat at the coffeehouse.
18. Coffeehouse partner with Matilda
19. Eloped with her French tutor
20. Hiding place for coffeehouse money

Fever 1793 Fill In The Blanks 4 Answer Key

BELLS	1. These ring whenever someone dies.
BATHE	2. Matilda does this once a month and on special occasions.
CART	3. A man dumps Matilda's mother off of one.
SWORD	4. Matilda stabs the robber with it.
MOTHER	5. She is assumed dead but comes back to the coffeehouse at the end.
WASHINGTON	6. Business grows when George ___ builds a home a few blocks away.
SKIRT	7. Matilda uses this to try to catch fish.
BIBLE	8. Matilda likes to read it at the end of each day.
SILAS	9. The cat's name
WAGON	10. Transportation to the country
COUNTRY	11. Wealthy people flee there to escape the fever.
ROBBED	12. Matilda and her grandfather return to Philadelphia & discover they were ___.
GEORGE	13. Parrot's name: King ___
OGLIVIE	14. Family Matilda's mother hopes her daughter can marry into
GARDEN	15. Place Matilda's grandfather wants her to get their food
FROST	16. It kills off the mosquitoes and the yellow fever.
JEFFERSON	17. Matilda wants to get Thomas ___ to eat at the coffeehouse.
ELIZA	18. Coffeehouse partner with Matilda
COLETTE	19. Eloped with her French tutor
STRONGBOX	20. Hiding place for coffeehouse money

Fever 1793 Matching 1

___ 1. ORPHANAGE A. Matilda wants to get Thomas ___ to eat at the coffeehouse.
___ 2. DOWRY B. These doctors know how to treat the fever better than anyone else.
___ 3. COUNTRY C. Chore to keep the children busy: ___ butter
___ 4. PORTRAIT D. Place where people buy and sell food
___ 5. BELLS E. Transportation to the country
___ 6. WILLOW F. Eliza's brother who lost his wife to yellow fever
___ 7. LUDINGTON G. Small child Matilda finds and cares for
___ 8. JOSEPH H. Matilda uses this to try to catch fish.
___ 9. WAGON I. Place the people at Bush Hill want Matilda to go to help out
___ 10. MARKET J. These ring whenever someone dies.
___ 11. PEALE K. She is assumed dead but comes back to the coffeehouse at the end.
___ 12. BATHE L. Parrot's name: King ___
___ 13. RUSH M. Joseph thinks Matilda should sell the coffeehouse so she has a nice ___.
___ 14. PRAYER N. Matilda is taken to ___ Hill to recover from yellow fever.
___ 15. CHURN O. Matilda does this once a month and on special occasions.
___ 16. MOTHER P. Wealthy people flee there to escape the fever.
___ 17. JEFFERSON Q. Family whose farm Matilda's mother wants to send her to
___ 18. BUSH R. Item Matilda buries with her grandfather
___ 19. NELL S. Matilda likes to read it at the end of each day.
___ 20. FRENCH T. He believes black people can't catch yellow fever.
___ 21. BIBLE U. Nathaniel Benson throws these out a window at Matilda and Eliza.
___ 22. FLOWERS V. Matilda's mother forbids her to go there for fear she might get sick.
___ 23. SKIRT W. Matilda has to fight to get one said at her grandfather's funeral.
___ 24. WHARVES X. Matilda searches for this kind of a tree, knowing water will be nearby.
___ 25. GEORGE Y. Nathaniel sends Matilda a note saying he is safe at ___'s house.

Fever 1793 Matching 1 Answer Key

I - 1. ORPHANAGE	A.	Matilda wants to get Thomas ___ to eat at the coffeehouse.
M - 2. DOWRY	B.	These doctors know how to treat the fever better than anyone else.
P - 3. COUNTRY	C.	Chore to keep the children busy: ___ butter
R - 4. PORTRAIT	D.	Place where people buy and sell food
J - 5. BELLS	E.	Transportation to the country
X - 6. WILLOW	F.	Eliza's brother who lost his wife to yellow fever
Q - 7. LUDINGTON	G.	Small child Matilda finds and cares for
F - 8. JOSEPH	H.	Matilda uses this to try to catch fish.
E - 9. WAGON	I.	Place the people at Bush Hill want Matilda to go to help out
D - 10. MARKET	J.	These ring whenever someone dies.
Y - 11. PEALE	K.	She is assumed dead but comes back to the coffeehouse at the end.
O - 12. BATHE	L.	Parrot's name: King ___
T - 13. RUSH	M.	Joseph thinks Matilda should sell the coffeehouse so she has a nice ___.
W - 14. PRAYER	N.	Matilda is taken to ___ Hill to recover from yellow fever.
C - 15. CHURN	O.	Matilda does this once a month and on special occasions.
K - 16. MOTHER	P.	Wealthy people flee there to escape the fever.
A - 17. JEFFERSON	Q.	Family whose farm Matilda's mother wants to send her to
N - 18. BUSH	R.	Item Matilda buries with her grandfather
G - 19. NELL	S.	Matilda likes to read it at the end of each day.
B - 20. FRENCH	T.	He believes black people can't catch yellow fever.
S - 21. BIBLE	U.	Nathaniel Benson throws these out a window at Matilda and Eliza.
U - 22. FLOWERS	V.	Matilda's mother forbids her to go there for fear she might get sick.
H - 23. SKIRT	W.	Matilda has to fight to get one said at her grandfather's funeral.
V - 24. WHARVES	X.	Matilda searches for this kind of a tree, knowing water will be nearby.
L - 25. GEORGE	Y.	Nathaniel sends Matilda a note saying he is safe at ___'s house.

Copyrighted

Fever 1793 Matching 2

___ 1. CHURN   A. Chore to keep the children busy: ___ butter
___ 2. FATHER   B. Item Matilda buries with her grandfather
___ 3. PRAYER   C. Coffeehouse partner with Matilda
___ 4. GARDEN   D. Matilda wants to get Thomas ___ to eat at the coffeehouse.
___ 5. BELLS   E. Parrot's name: King ___
___ 6. WAGON   F. Family whose farm Matilda's mother wants to send her to
___ 7. GEORGE   G. Matilda is gathering these when she passes out, sick with the fever
___ 8. WHARVES   H. Matilda likes to read it at the end of each day.
___ 9. CART   I. Eliza's brother who lost his wife to yellow fever
___ 10. PORTRAIT   J. These ring whenever someone dies.
___ 11. DOWRY   K. A man dumps Matilda's mother off of one.
___ 12. FRENCH   L. Hiding place for coffeehouse money
___ 13. ELIZA   M. People mixed it with flour to make more bread.
___ 14. JEFFERSON   N. Family Matilda's mother hopes her daughter can marry into
___ 15. PEARS   O. These doctors know how to treat the fever better than anyone else.
___ 16. BIBLE   P. Matilda's mother forbids her to go there for fear she might get sick.
___ 17. LUDINGTON   Q. He fell off a ladder and died of a broken neck.
___ 18. NELL   R. Small child Matilda finds and cares for
___ 19. JOSEPH   S. Joseph thinks Matilda should sell the coffeehouse so she has a nice ___.
___ 20. FLAGG   T. Matilda has to fight to get one said at her grandfather's funeral.
___ 21. STRONGBOX   U. What Matilda and Nathaniel do every evening
___ 22. WALK   V. Country Matilda wants to go to
___ 23. FRANCE   W. Transportation to the country
___ 24. OGLIVIE   X. Grandfather flirts with her as she nurses Matilda back to health.
___ 25. SAWDUST   Y. Place Matilda's grandfather wants her to get their food

Fever 1793 Matching 2 Answer Key

A - 1. CHURN	A.	Chore to keep the children busy: ___ butter
Q - 2. FATHER	B.	Item Matilda buries with her grandfather
T - 3. PRAYER	C.	Coffeehouse partner with Matilda
Y - 4. GARDEN	D.	Matilda wants to get Thomas ___ to eat at the coffeehouse.
J - 5. BELLS	E.	Parrot's name: King ___
W - 6. WAGON	F.	Family whose farm Matilda's mother wants to send her to
E - 7. GEORGE	G.	Matilda is gathering these when she passes out, sick with the fever
P - 8. WHARVES	H.	Matilda likes to read it at the end of each day.
K - 9. CART	I.	Eliza's brother who lost his wife to yellow fever
B - 10. PORTRAIT	J.	These ring whenever someone dies.
S - 11. DOWRY	K.	A man dumps Matilda's mother off of one.
O - 12. FRENCH	L.	Hiding place for coffeehouse money
C - 13. ELIZA	M.	People mixed it with flour to make more bread.
D - 14. JEFFERSON	N.	Family Matilda's mother hopes her daughter can marry into
G - 15. PEARS	O.	These doctors know how to treat the fever better than anyone else.
H - 16. BIBLE	P.	Matilda's mother forbids her to go there for fear she might get sick.
F - 17. LUDINGTON	Q.	He fell off a ladder and died of a broken neck.
R - 18. NELL	R.	Small child Matilda finds and cares for
I - 19. JOSEPH	S.	Joseph thinks Matilda should sell the coffeehouse so she has a nice ___.
X - 20. FLAGG	T.	Matilda has to fight to get one said at her grandfather's funeral.
L - 21. STRONGBOX	U.	What Matilda and Nathaniel do every evening
U - 22. WALK	V.	Country Matilda wants to go to
V - 23. FRANCE	W.	Transportation to the country
N - 24. OGLIVIE	X.	Grandfather flirts with her as she nurses Matilda back to health.
M - 25. SAWDUST	Y.	Place Matilda's grandfather wants her to get their food

Fever 1793 Matching 3

___ 1. SAWDUST   A. The cat's name
___ 2. SKIRT   B. Country Matilda wants to go to
___ 3. SWORD   C. Matilda likes to read it at the end of each day.
___ 4. ROBBED   D. Item Matilda buries with her grandfather
___ 5. MARKET   E. Nathaniel Benson's job
___ 6. WILLOW   F. Matilda is gathering these when she passes out, sick with the fever
___ 7. BUSH   G. He believes black people can't catch yellow fever.
___ 8. WAGON   H. Stephen ___ turns Bush Hill into a safe hospital.
___ 9. ELIZA   I. Author
___ 10. RUSH   J. People mixed it with flour to make more bread.
___ 11. CHURN   K. Parrot's name: King ___
___ 12. WALK   L. Matilda is taken to ___ Hill to recover from yellow fever.
___ 13. FRANCE   M. Family whose farm Matilda's mother wants to send her to
___ 14. PORTRAIT   N. Coffeehouse partner with Matilda
___ 15. PRAYER   O. Matilda searches for this kind of a tree, knowing water will be nearby.
___ 16. PAINTER   P. Matilda stabs the robber with it.
___ 17. BIBLE   Q. Matilda and her grandfather return to Philadelphia & discover they were ___.
___ 18. ANDERSON   R. Chore to keep the children busy: ___ butter
___ 19. LUDINGTON   S. Transportation to the country
___ 20. PEARS   T. Girl who worked at the coffeehouse who dies of yellow fever
___ 21. FLOWERS   U. Place where people buy and sell food
___ 22. SILAS   V. Matilda has to fight to get one said at her grandfather's funeral.
___ 23. GIRARD   W. Matilda uses this to try to catch fish.
___ 24. POLLY   X. What Matilda and Nathaniel do every evening
___ 25. GEORGE   Y. Nathaniel Benson throws these out a window at Matilda and Eliza.

Fever 1793 Matching 3 Answer Key

J - 1. SAWDUST	A.	The cat's name
W - 2. SKIRT	B.	Country Matilda wants to go to
P - 3. SWORD	C.	Matilda likes to read it at the end of each day.
Q - 4. ROBBED	D.	Item Matilda buries with her grandfather
U - 5. MARKET	E.	Nathaniel Benson's job
O - 6. WILLOW	F.	Matilda is gathering these when she passes out, sick with the fever
L - 7. BUSH	G.	He believes black people can't catch yellow fever.
S - 8. WAGON	H.	Stephen ___ turns Bush Hill into a safe hospital.
N - 9. ELIZA	I.	Author
G -10. RUSH	J.	People mixed it with flour to make more bread.
R -11. CHURN	K.	Parrot's name: King ___
X -12. WALK	L.	Matilda is taken to ___ Hill to recover from yellow fever.
B -13. FRANCE	M.	Family whose farm Matilda's mother wants to send her to
D -14. PORTRAIT	N.	Coffeehouse partner with Matilda
V -15. PRAYER	O.	Matilda searches for this kind of a tree, knowing water will be nearby.
E -16. PAINTER	P.	Matilda stabs the robber with it.
C -17. BIBLE	Q.	Matilda and her grandfather return to Philadelphia & discover they were ___.
I - 18. ANDERSON	R.	Chore to keep the children busy: ___ butter
M -19. LUDINGTON	S.	Transportation to the country
F -20. PEARS	T.	Girl who worked at the coffeehouse who dies of yellow fever
Y -21. FLOWERS	U.	Place where people buy and sell food
A -22. SILAS	V.	Matilda has to fight to get one said at her grandfather's funeral.
H -23. GIRARD	W.	Matilda uses this to try to catch fish.
T -24. POLLY	X.	What Matilda and Nathaniel do every evening
K -25. GEORGE	Y.	Nathaniel Benson throws these out a window at Matilda and Eliza.

Fever 1793 Matching 4

___ 1. LUDINGTON A. She is assumed dead but comes back to the coffeehouse at the end.
___ 2. GARDEN B. Family whose farm Matilda's mother wants to send her to
___ 3. FLAGG C. It kills off the mosquitoes and the yellow fever.
___ 4. FROST D. Matilda is gathering these when she passes out, sick with the fever
___ 5. ELIZA E. The cat's name
___ 6. PAINTER F. Matilda stabs the robber with it.
___ 7. CART G. A man dumps Matilda's mother off of one.
___ 8. PORTRAIT H. Matilda and her grandfather return to Philadelphia & discover they were ___.
___ 9. PRAYER I. Hiding place for coffeehouse money
___ 10. ROBBED J. Matilda wants to get Thomas ___ to eat at the coffeehouse.
___ 11. GEORGE K. Item Matilda buries with her grandfather
___ 12. SILAS L. Parrot's name: King ___
___ 13. SWORD M. Place Matilda's grandfather wants her to get their food
___ 14. JEFFERSON N. Matilda has to fight to get one said at her grandfather's funeral.
___ 15. FRENCH O. He fell off a ladder and died of a broken neck.
___ 16. WHARVES P. These doctors know how to treat the fever better than anyone else.
___ 17. WALK Q. Matilda does this once a month and on special occasions.
___ 18. PEARS R. Author
___ 19. STRONGBOX S. Transportation to the country
___ 20. WAGON T. Family Matilda's mother hopes her daughter can marry into
___ 21. ANDERSON U. Grandfather flirts with her as she nurses Matilda back to health.
___ 22. FATHER V. Coffeehouse partner with Matilda
___ 23. MOTHER W. Nathaniel Benson's job
___ 24. OGLIVIE X. What Matilda and Nathaniel do every evening
___ 25. BATHE Y. Matilda's mother forbids her to go there for fear she might get sick.

Fever 1793 Matching 4 Answer Key

B - 1. LUDINGTON	A. She is assumed dead but comes back to the coffeehouse at the end.
M - 2. GARDEN	B. Family whose farm Matilda's mother wants to send her to
U - 3. FLAGG	C. It kills off the mosquitoes and the yellow fever.
C - 4. FROST	D. Matilda is gathering these when she passes out, sick with the fever
V - 5. ELIZA	E. The cat's name
W - 6. PAINTER	F. Matilda stabs the robber with it.
G - 7. CART	G. A man dumps Matilda's mother off of one.
K - 8. PORTRAIT	H. Matilda and her grandfather return to Philadelphia & discover they were ___.
N - 9. PRAYER	I. Hiding place for coffeehouse money
H - 10. ROBBED	J. Matilda wants to get Thomas ___ to eat at the coffeehouse.
L - 11. GEORGE	K. Item Matilda buries with her grandfather
E - 12. SILAS	L. Parrot's name: King ___
F - 13. SWORD	M. Place Matilda's grandfather wants her to get their food
J - 14. JEFFERSON	N. Matilda has to fight to get one said at her grandfather's funeral.
P - 15. FRENCH	O. He fell off a ladder and died of a broken neck.
Y - 16. WHARVES	P. These doctors know how to treat the fever better than anyone else.
X - 17. WALK	Q. Matilda does this once a month and on special occasions.
D - 18. PEARS	R. Author
I - 19. STRONGBOX	S. Transportation to the country
S - 20. WAGON	T. Family Matilda's mother hopes her daughter can marry into
R - 21. ANDERSON	U. Grandfather flirts with her as she nurses Matilda back to health.
O - 22. FATHER	V. Coffeehouse partner with Matilda
A - 23. MOTHER	W. Nathaniel Benson's job
T - 24. OGLIVIE	X. What Matilda and Nathaniel do every evening
Q - 25. BATHE	Y. Matilda's mother forbids her to go there for fear she might get sick.

Fever 1793 Magic Squares 1

Match the definition with the vocabulary word. Put your answers in the magic squares below. When your answers are correct, all columns and rows will add to the same number.

A. FLOWERS
B. PRAYER
C. POLLY
D. SAWDUST
E. BIBLE
F. PEALE
G. PORTRAIT
H. WILLOW
I. BUSH
J. FATHER
K. SILAS
L. ELIZA
M. ANDERSON
N. WHARVES
O. LUDINGTON
P. SKIRT

1. Nathaniel Benson throws these out a window at Matilda and Eliza.
2. Matilda's mother forbids her to go there for fear she might get sick.
3. He fell off a ladder and died of a broken neck.
4. Matilda likes to read it at the end of each day.
5. Item Matilda buries with her grandfather
6. Coffeehouse partner with Matilda
7. Matilda uses this to try to catch fish.
8. Girl who worked at the coffeehouse who dies of yellow fever
9. Family whose farm Matilda's mother wants to send her to
10. People mixed it with flour to make more bread.
11. Matilda searches for this kind of a tree, knowing water will be nearby.
12. The cat's name
13. Matilda is taken to ___ Hill to recover from yellow fever.
14. Nathaniel sends Matilda a note saying he is safe at ___'s house.
15. Matilda has to fight to get one said at her grandfather's funeral.
16. Author

A=	B=	C=	D=
E=	F=	G=	H=
I=	J=	K=	L=
M=	N=	O=	P=

Fever 1793 Magic Squares 1 Answer Key

Match the definition with the vocabulary word. Put your answers in the magic squares below. When your answers are correct, all columns and rows will add to the same number.

A. FLOWERS
B. PRAYER
C. POLLY
D. SAWDUST
E. BIBLE
F. PEALE
G. PORTRAIT
H. WILLOW
I. BUSH
J. FATHER
K. SILAS
L. ELIZA
M. ANDERSON
N. WHARVES
O. LUDINGTON
P. SKIRT

1. Nathaniel Benson throws these out a window at Matilda and Eliza.
2. Matilda's mother forbids her to go there for fear she might get sick.
3. He fell off a ladder and died of a broken neck.
4. Matilda likes to read it at the end of each day.
5. Item Matilda buries with her grandfather
6. Coffeehouse partner with Matilda
7. Matilda uses this to try to catch fish.
8. Girl who worked at the coffeehouse who dies of yellow fever
9. Family whose farm Matilda's mother wants to send her to
10. People mixed it with flour to make more bread.
11. Matilda searches for this kind of a tree, knowing water will be nearby.
12. The cat's name
13. Matilda is taken to ___ Hill to recover from yellow fever.
14. Nathaniel sends Matilda a note saying he is safe at ___'s house.
15. Matilda has to fight to get one said at her grandfather's funeral.
16. Author

A=1	B=15	C=8	D=10
E=4	F=14	G=5	H=11
I=13	J=3	K=12	L=6
M=16	N=2	O=9	P=7

Fever 1793 Magic Squares 2

Match the definition with the vocabulary word. Put your answers in the magic squares below. When your answers are correct, all columns and rows will add to the same number.

A. JEFFERSON E. MOTHER I. BATHE M. DOWRY
B. SKIRT F. ELIZA J. WHARVES N. STRONGBOX
C. NELL G. RUSH K. PEARS O. FLOWERS
D. PORTRAIT H. ORPHANAGE L. FATHER P. BELLS

1. Joseph thinks Matilda should sell the coffeehouse so she has a nice ___.
2. Coffeehouse partner with Matilda
3. Place the people at Bush Hill want Matilda to go to help out
4. Nathaniel Benson throws these out a window at Matilda and Eliza.
5. He fell off a ladder and died of a broken neck.
6. Small child Matilda finds and cares for
7. Matilda wants to get Thomas ___ to eat at the coffeehouse.
8. Matilda's mother forbids her to go there for fear she might get sick.
9. Matilda is gathering these when she passes out, sick with the fever
10. Item Matilda buries with her grandfather
11. Matilda uses this to try to catch fish.
12. Matilda does this once a month and on special occasions.
13. Hiding place for coffeehouse money
14. She is assumed dead but comes back to the coffeehouse at the end.
15. He believes black people can't catch yellow fever.
16. These ring whenever someone dies.

A= 7	B= 11	C= 6	D= 10
E= 14	F= 2	G= 15	H= 3
I= 12	J= 8	K= 9	L= 5
M= 1	N= 13	O= 4	P= 16

Fever 1793 Magic Squares 2 Answer Key

Match the definition with the vocabulary word. Put your answers in the magic squares below. When your answers are correct, all columns and rows will add to the same number.

A. JEFFERSON E. MOTHER   I. BATHE   M. DOWRY
B. SKIRT   F. ELIZA   J. WHARVES N. STRONGBOX
C. NELL   G. RUSH   K. PEARS   O. FLOWERS
D. PORTRAIT   H. ORPHANAGE L. FATHER   P. BELLS

1. Joseph thinks Matilda should sell the coffeehouse so she has a nice ___.
2. Coffeehouse partner with Matilda
3. Place the people at Bush Hill want Matilda to go to help out
4. Nathaniel Benson throws these out a window at Matilda and Eliza.
5. He fell off a ladder and died of a broken neck.
6. Small child Matilda finds and cares for
7. Matilda wants to get Thomas ___ to eat at the coffeehouse.
8. Matilda's mother forbids her to go there for fear she might get sick.
9. Matilda is gathering these when she passes out, sick with the fever
10. Item Matilda buries with her grandfather
11. Matilda uses this to try to catch fish.
12. Matilda does this once a month and on special occasions.
13. Hiding place for coffeehouse money
14. She is assumed dead but comes back to the coffeehouse at the end.
15. He believes black people can't catch yellow fever.
16. These ring whenever someone dies.

A=7	B=11	C=6	D=10
E=14	F=2	G=15	H=3
I=12	J=8	K=9	L=5
M=1	N=13	O=4	P=16

Fever 1793 Magic Squares 3

Match the definition with the vocabulary word. Put your answers in the magic squares below. When your answers are correct, all columns and rows will add to the same number.

A. NELL
B. PRAYER
C. CART
D. JOSEPH
E. FATHER
F. BUSH
G. GEORGE
H. FLAGG
I. ROBBED
J. COUNTRY
K. WHARVES
L. SWORD
M. MOTHER
N. REFUGEES
O. SILAS
P. WILLOW

1. Matilda has to fight to get one said at her grandfather's funeral.
2. Parrot's name: King ___
3. Matilda's mother forbids her to go there for fear she might get sick.
4. People Matilda's grandfather thinks are to blame for the fever
5. She is assumed dead but comes back to the coffeehouse at the end.
6. Matilda stabs the robber with it.
7. Grandfather flirts with her as she nurses Matilda back to health.
8. Small child Matilda finds and cares for
9. Matilda searches for this kind of a tree, knowing water will be nearby.
10. Matilda and her grandfather return to Philadelphia & discover they were ___.
11. He fell off a ladder and died of a broken neck.
12. Eliza's brother who lost his wife to yellow fever
13. A man dumps Matilda's mother off of one.
14. Matilda is taken to ___ Hill to recover from yellow fever.
15. Wealthy people flee there to escape the fever.
16. The cat's name

A=	B=	C=	D=
E=	F=	G=	H=
I=	J=	K=	L=
M=	N=	O=	P=

Fever 1793 Magic Squares 3 Answer Key

Match the definition with the vocabulary word. Put your answers in the magic squares below. When your answers are correct, all columns and rows will add to the same number.

A. NELL
B. PRAYER
C. CART
D. JOSEPH
E. FATHER
F. BUSH
G. GEORGE
H. FLAGG
I. ROBBED
J. COUNTRY
K. WHARVES
L. SWORD
M. MOTHER
N. REFUGEES
O. SILAS
P. WILLOW

1. Matilda has to fight to get one said at her grandfather's funeral.
2. Parrot's name: King ___
3. Matilda's mother forbids her to go there for fear she might get sick.
4. People Matilda's grandfather thinks are to blame for the fever
5. She is assumed dead but comes back to the coffeehouse at the end.
6. Matilda stabs the robber with it.
7. Grandfather flirts with her as she nurses Matilda back to health.
8. Small child Matilda finds and cares for
9. Matilda searches for this kind of a tree, knowing water will be nearby.
10. Matilda and her grandfather return to Philadelphia & discover they were ___.
11. He fell off a ladder and died of a broken neck.
12. Eliza's brother who lost his wife to yellow fever
13. A man dumps Matilda's mother off of one.
14. Matilda is taken to ___ Hill to recover from yellow fever.
15. Wealthy people flee there to escape the fever.
16. The cat's name

A=8	B=1	C=13	D=12
E=11	F=14	G=2	H=7
I=10	J=15	K=3	L=6
M=5	N=4	O=16	P=9

Fever 1793 Magic Squares 4

Match the definition with the vocabulary word. Put your answers in the magic squares below. When your answers are correct, all columns and rows will add to the same number.

A. GARDEN
B. GIRARD
C. ORPHANAGE
D. CHURN
E. WILLOW
F. COLETTE
G. MOTHER
H. BUSH
I. FLAGG
J. FLOWERS
K. MARKET
L. JOSEPH
M. WAGON
N. RUSH
O. ELIZA
P. FRENCH

1. Matilda is taken to ___ Hill to recover from yellow fever.
2. Place Matilda's grandfather wants her to get their food
3. Stephen ___ turns Bush Hill into a safe hospital.
4. She is assumed dead but comes back to the coffeehouse at the end.
5. Nathaniel Benson throws these out a window at Matilda and Eliza.
6. Coffeehouse partner with Matilda
7. These doctors know how to treat the fever better than anyone else.
8. Grandfather flirts with her as she nurses Matilda back to health.
9. Place where people buy and sell food
10. He believes black people can't catch yellow fever.
11. Transportation to the country
12. Eliza's brother who lost his wife to yellow fever
13. Matilda searches for this kind of a tree, knowing water will be nearby.
14. Chore to keep the children busy: ___ butter
15. Place the people at Bush Hill want Matilda to go to help out
16. Eloped with her French tutor

A=	B=	C=	D=
E=	F=	G=	H=
I=	J=	K=	L=
M=	N=	O=	P=

Fever 1793 Magic Squares 4 Answer Key

Match the definition with the vocabulary word. Put your answers in the magic squares below. When your answers are correct, all columns and rows will add to the same number.

A. GARDEN
B. GIRARD
C. ORPHANAGE
D. CHURN
E. WILLOW
F. COLETTE
G. MOTHER
H. BUSH
I. FLAGG
J. FLOWERS
K. MARKET
L. JOSEPH
M. WAGON
N. RUSH
O. ELIZA
P. FRENCH

1. Matilda is taken to ___ Hill to recover from yellow fever.
2. Place Matilda's grandfather wants her to get their food
3. Stephen ___ turns Bush Hill into a safe hospital.
4. She is assumed dead but comes back to the coffeehouse at the end.
5. Nathaniel Benson throws these out a window at Matilda and Eliza.
6. Coffeehouse partner with Matilda
7. These doctors know how to treat the fever better than anyone else.
8. Grandfather flirts with her as she nurses Matilda back to health.
9. Place where people buy and sell food
10. He believes black people can't catch yellow fever.
11. Transportation to the country
12. Eliza's brother who lost his wife to yellow fever
13. Matilda searches for this kind of a tree, knowing water will be nearby.
14. Chore to keep the children busy: ___ butter
15. Place the people at Bush Hill want Matilda to go to help out
16. Eloped with her French tutor

A=2	B=3	C=15	D=14
E=13	F=16	G=4	H=1
I=8	J=5	K=9	L=12
M=11	N=10	O=6	P=7

Fever 1793 Word Search 1

```
J O S E P H L B I B L E G H G N F P T
K Z Z R R L A U J W R G S I E L E O N
F D K Y E T O S Z W A U R V O A P R J
R N D N H C G H B L R A A W R P O P E
C O T E T J L C F W R Z E S G A R H F
B O B J A M I A V D I R X S E I T A F
C N U B F J V R K L S S A D S N R N E
Z O B N E S I T E R T W P M D T A A R
P T L R T D E B P R D O A O A E I G S
X G X E V R W H I U Y R D L L R T E O
Y N C Y T L Y K S B A D L G K L K Y N
V I M H Z T S T G F N B E L L S Y E Z
X D L O U P E N J D D R Q D W D R R T
C U S Q T R S D J P E G P I N P E H G
E L A E P H N O V Y R P L W V F S C F
K N S D Q C E W A X S L S A U C V N J
F D I E C N A R F R O S T G A R D E N
R M L X F B P Y K W N S E O R L P R B
W H A R V E S C C F F E G N T G R F V
W A S H I N G T O N S T R O N G B O X
```

ANDERSON	ELIZA	JEFFERSON	PEARS	STRONGBOX
BATHE	FATHER	JOSEPH	POLLY	SWORD
BELLS	FLAGG	LUDINGTON	PORTRAIT	WAGON
BIBLE	FLOWERS	MARKET	PRAYER	WALK
BUSH	FRANCE	MOTHER	REFUGEES	WASHINGTON
CART	FRENCH	NELL	ROBBED	WHARVES
CHURN	FROST	OGLIVIE	RUSH	WILLOW
COLETTE	GARDEN	ORPHANAGE	SAWDUST	
COUNTRY	GEORGE	PAINTER	SILAS	
DOWRY	GIRARD	PEALE	SKIRT	

Fever 1793 Word Search 1 Answer Key

```
  J O S E P H L B I B L E G H G   F P
        R L       A       S I E   E O
        E A       U       G   L   O R
    R   T O   S   R       S   E   P J
    C O N H   H   A       A   P A P E
    O O E T   C F R       W R G A O F
      B   A   A   Z E     S E   I R F
    C N   F   R   D I R S   A   N P E
      U   B   I   L S A     T   T H R
    N   B E   T E   T W P M O   R A S
    O     D   R   R D O A O A   A N O
    T L   E   I   I R L R L R   I G N
    G   T     Y K S   A D   K   T E
    N C H     T S T   N B E L L S Y
    I M O       E     D R     W   E
    D O U       D       I     E   R T
    U T R       N       L W   F   H
  E L A E P   N O Y R   A U     C
    S     H   E W A S L   G     N
    I E C N A R F R O S T A R D E N
    L     P   E   Y W N   E O   R
  W H A R V E S       E   N     F
  W A S H I N G T O N S T R O N G B O X
```

ANDERSON	ELIZA	JEFFERSON	PEARS	STRONGBOX
BATHE	FATHER	JOSEPH	POLLY	SWORD
BELLS	FLAGG	LUDINGTON	PORTRAIT	WAGON
BIBLE	FLOWERS	MARKET	PRAYER	WALK
BUSH	FRANCE	MOTHER	REFUGEES	WASHINGTON
CART	FRENCH	NELL	ROBBED	WHARVES
CHURN	FROST	OGLIVIE	RUSH	WILLOW
COLETTE	GARDEN	ORPHANAGE	SAWDUST	
COUNTRY	GEORGE	PAINTER	SILAS	
DOWRY	GIRARD	PEALE	SKIRT	

Fever 1793 Word Search 2

```
W D O W R Y O G L I V I E B G Y P F O
L A T B I G B N I F K S H I A O M L R
S U G B Q L E T R R S J B B L T R O P
T R D O B B L M Q E A Z Z L F G H W H
R P T I N P L O V N F R Y E R A C E A
O B S F N C S R W C P U D M A R O R N
N R U H C G A N P H J R G W N D L S A
G W D P N H T S G P E P A E C E E N G
B A W E W B H O V D F S L Y E N T W E
O S A S W F L S N T F D Y R E S T M R
X H S O R O B B E D E C D G S R E O D
V I P J W Y Y M Z C R W B J I Z H T R
C N O K S A L A R O S N B B L X N H H
E G R O E G L R S U O R H U A O C E T
H T T F T R I K S N N Y J S S W O R D
B O R P A R F E P T Y H E R B H A H G
V N A Z K L U T T R Y L E A C C Z G H
P A I N T E R S C Y A D N E L L A B Y
X L T R P L M P H E N W Z P Q L V X S
E F A T H E R W P A R M M D F R O S T
```

ANDERSON	ELIZA	JEFFERSON	PEARS	STRONGBOX
BATHE	FATHER	JOSEPH	POLLY	SWORD
BELLS	FLAGG	LUDINGTON	PORTRAIT	WAGON
BIBLE	FLOWERS	MARKET	PRAYER	WALK
BUSH	FRANCE	MOTHER	REFUGEES	WASHINGTON
CART	FRENCH	NELL	ROBBED	WHARVES
CHURN	FROST	OGLIVIE	RUSH	WILLOW
COLETTE	GARDEN	ORPHANAGE	SAWDUST	
COUNTRY	GEORGE	PAINTER	SILAS	
DOWRY	GIRARD	PEALE	SKIRT	

Fever 1793 Word Search 2 Answer Key

ANDERSON	ELIZA	JEFFERSON	PEARS	STRONGBOX
BATHE	FATHER	JOSEPH	POLLY	SWORD
BELLS	FLAGG	LUDINGTON	PORTRAIT	WAGON
BIBLE	FLOWERS	MARKET	PRAYER	WALK
BUSH	FRANCE	MOTHER	REFUGEES	WASHINGTON
CART	FRENCH	NELL	ROBBED	WHARVES
CHURN	FROST	OGLIVIE	RUSH	WILLOW
COLETTE	GARDEN	ORPHANAGE	SAWDUST	
COUNTRY	GEORGE	PAINTER	SILAS	
DOWRY	GIRARD	PEALE	SKIRT	

Fever 1793 Word Search 3

```
J F L O W E R S P O R T R A I T N B
B O D V A L P Y O H Q B E L L S Y S
Z T S X L W E B L H Z I T S H O R F
F D J E K J A G L W O B N F N R E L
R U S H P W L G Y I R L I X L F F Z
C K H W G H E A H L P E A S Z A U Q
S H N C L E Y R M L H P P I R L G T
T D U A G G J D R O A S E L F F E G
R Q R R O B B E D W N W H A R V E S
O X O T N N H N F O A W T S R T S G
N E E R L T Y F S F G H A N T S X M
G L I W O X P R A Y E R B E N M K D
B I V M M J E A B R T R L Y K A Y C
O Z I L T D B N D N M O S N F R B R
X A L W N Y K C S P C G N O W K U B
K E G A J F R E W A G O N O N E S Y
N N O T G N I D U L J D D J M T H X
```

A man dumps Matilda's mother off of one. (4)
Author (8)
Chore to keep the children busy: ___ butter (5)
Coffeehouse partner with Matilda (5)
Country Matilda wants to go to (6)
Eliza's brother who lost his wife to yellow fever (6)
Eloped with her French tutor (7)
Family Matilda's mother hopes her daughter can marry into (7)
Family whose farm Matilda's mother wants to send her to (9)
Girl who worked at the coffeehouse who dies of yellow fever (5)
Grandfather flirts with her as she nurses Matilda back to health. (5)
He believes black people can't catch yellow fever. (4)
He fell off a ladder and died of a broken neck. (6)
Hiding place for coffeehouse money (9)
It kills off the mosquitoes and the yellow fever. (5)
Item Matilda buries with her grandfather (8)
Joseph thinks Matilda should sell the coffeehouse so she has a nice ___. (5)
Matilda and her grandfather return to Philadelphia & discover they were ___. (6)
Matilda does this once a month and on special occasions. (5)
Matilda has to fight to get one said at her grandfather's funeral. (6)
Matilda is gathering these when she passes out, sick with the fever (5)
Matilda is taken to ___ Hill to recover from yellow fever. (4)
Matilda likes to read it at the end of each day. (5)
Matilda searches for this kind of a tree, knowing water will be nearby. (6)
Matilda wants to get Thomas ___ to eat at the coffeehouse. (9)
Matilda's mother forbids her to go there for fear she might get sick. (7)
Nathaniel Benson throws these out a window at Matilda and Eliza. (7)
Nathaniel Benson's job (7)
Nathaniel sends Matilda a note saying he is safe at ___'s house. (5)
Parrot's name: King ___ (6)
People Matilda's grandfather thinks are to blame for the fever (8)
Place Matilda's grandfather wants her to get their food (6)
Place the people at Bush Hill want Matilda to go to help out (9)
Place where people buy and sell food (6)
She is assumed dead but comes back to the coffeehouse at the end. (6)
Small child Matilda finds and cares for (4)
The cat's name (5)
These ring whenever someone dies. (5)
Transportation to the country (5)
What Matilda and Nathaniel do every evening (4)

Fever 1793 Word Search 3 Answer Key

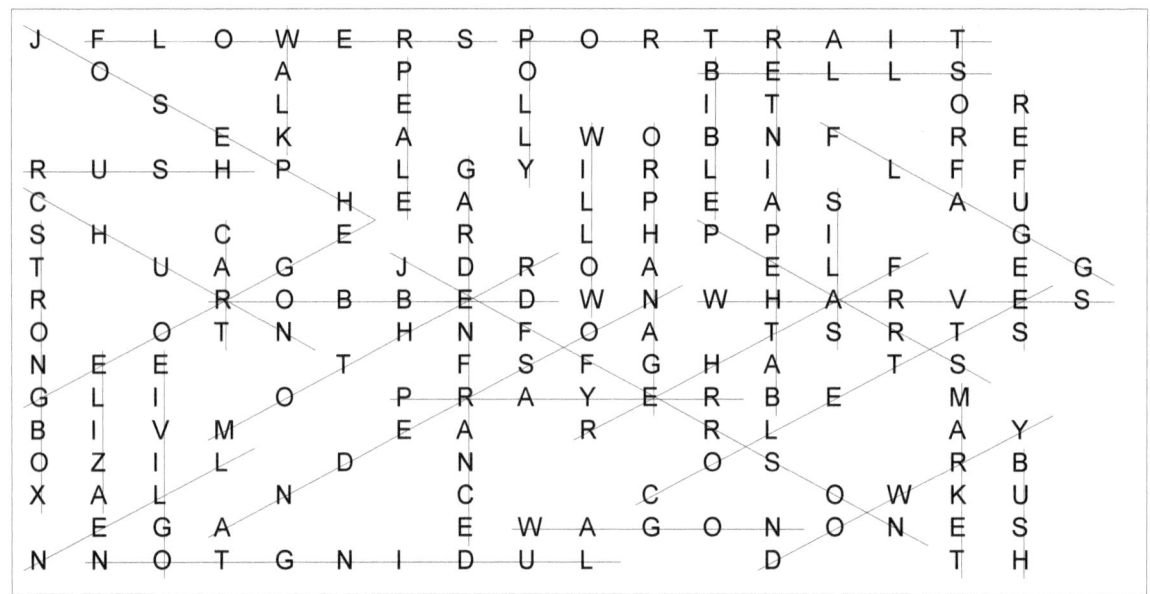

A man dumps Matilda's mother off of one. (4)
Author (8)
Chore to keep the children busy: ___ butter (5)
Coffeehouse partner with Matilda (5)
Country Matilda wants to go to (6)
Eliza's brother who lost his wife to yellow fever (6)
Eloped with her French tutor (7)
Family Matilda's mother hopes her daughter can marry into (7)
Family whose farm Matilda's mother wants to send her to (9)
Girl who worked at the coffeehouse who dies of yellow fever (5)
Grandfather flirts with her as she nurses Matilda back to health. (5)
He believes black people can't catch yellow fever. (4)
He fell off a ladder and died of a broken neck. (6)
Hiding place for coffeehouse money (9)
It kills off the mosquitoes and the yellow fever. (5)
Item Matilda buries with her grandfather (8)
Joseph thinks Matilda should sell the coffeehouse so she has a nice ___. (5)
Matilda and her grandfather return to Philadelphia & discover they were ___. (6)
Matilda does this once a month and on special occasions. (5)
Matilda has to fight to get one said at her grandfather's funeral. (6)
Matilda is gathering these when she passes out, sick with the fever (5)

Matilda is taken to ___ Hill to recover from yellow fever. (4)
Matilda likes to read it at the end of each day. (5)
Matilda searches for this kind of a tree, knowing water will be nearby. (6)
Matilda wants to get Thomas ___ to eat at the coffeehouse. (9)
Matilda's mother forbids her to go there for fear she might get sick. (7)
Nathaniel Benson throws these out a window at Matilda and Eliza. (7)
Nathaniel Benson's job (7)
Nathaniel sends Matilda a note saying he is safe at ___'s house. (5)
Parrot's name: King ___ (6)
People Matilda's grandfather thinks are to blame for the fever (8)
Place Matilda's grandfather wants her to get their food (6)
Place the people at Bush Hill want Matilda to go to help out (9)
Place where people buy and sell food (6)
She is assumed dead but comes back to the coffeehouse at the end. (6)
Small child Matilda finds and cares for (4)
The cat's name (5)
These ring whenever someone dies. (5)
Transportation to the country (5)
What Matilda and Nathaniel do every evening (4)

Fever 1793 Word Search 4

```
G E O R G E X S K I R T P P G W B G
Y M P T I C I L W J M A O R A I U J
D W R P R L S L N O I Y L A R L S C
H A R B A S F E D N R Y L Y D L H M
C B J S R G S B T Y F D Y E E O R G
N V S A D R T E R C R V J R N W U M
E C E W E C R W M O O B V O D Q S Z
R P X H A L O P R L S Z I B A T H E
F E T A N D N U Q E T W F B P T Q M
H A F R D E G P N T F L L E L D S G
F L V E L B Z W T R U A D T E G K
J E O E R I O Q A E R O G L I V I E
R T W S S Z X Q G J M Y G E Q Q C Z
Z W E L O A W L O G P L N N E H H X
G F R A N C E A N M O T H E R S U X
P T S U D W A S L G R Y G C L D R C
J O S E P H M A R K E T S X T L N P
```

- A man dumps Matilda's mother off of one. (4)
- Author (8)
- Chore to keep the children busy: ___ butter (5)
- Coffeehouse partner with Matilda (5)
- Country Matilda wants to go to (6)
- Eliza's brother who lost his wife to yellow fever (6)
- Eloped with her French tutor (7)
- Family Matilda's mother hopes her daughter can marry into (7)
- Girl who worked at the coffeehouse who dies of yellow fever (5)
- Grandfather flirts with her as she nurses Matilda back to health. (5)
- He believes black people can't catch yellow fever. (4)
- He fell off a ladder and died of a broken neck. (6)
- Hiding place for coffeehouse money (9)
- It kills off the mosquitoes and the yellow fever. (5)
- Joseph thinks Matilda should sell the coffeehouse so she has a nice ___. (5)
- Matilda and her grandfather return to Philadelphia & discover they were ___. (6)
- Matilda does this once a month and on special occasions. (5)
- Matilda has to fight to get one said at her grandfather's funeral. (6)
- Matilda is gathering these when she passes out, sick with the fever (5)
- Matilda is taken to ___ Hill to recover from yellow fever. (4)
- Matilda likes to read it at the end of each day. (5)
- Matilda searches for this kind of a tree, knowing water will be nearby. (6)
- Matilda stabs the robber with it. (5)
- Matilda uses this to try to catch fish. (5)
- Matilda's mother forbids her to go there for fear she might get sick. (7)
- Nathaniel Benson throws these out a window at Matilda and Eliza. (7)
- Nathaniel Benson's job (7)
- Nathaniel sends Matilda a note saying he is safe at ___'s house. (5)
- Parrot's name: King ___ (6)
- People Matilda's grandfather thinks are to blame for the fever (8)
- People mixed it with flour to make more bread. (7)
- Place Matilda's grandfather wants her to get their food (6)
- Place where people buy and sell food (6)
- She is assumed dead but comes back to the coffeehouse at the end. (6)
- Small child Matilda finds and cares for (4)
- Stephen ___ turns Bush Hill into a safe hospital. (6)
- The cat's name (5)
- These doctors know how to treat the fever better than anyone else. (6)
- These ring whenever someone dies. (5)
- Transportation to the country (5)
- Wealthy people flee there to escape the fever. (7)
- What Matilda and Nathaniel do every evening (4)

Fever 1793 Word Search 4 Answer Key

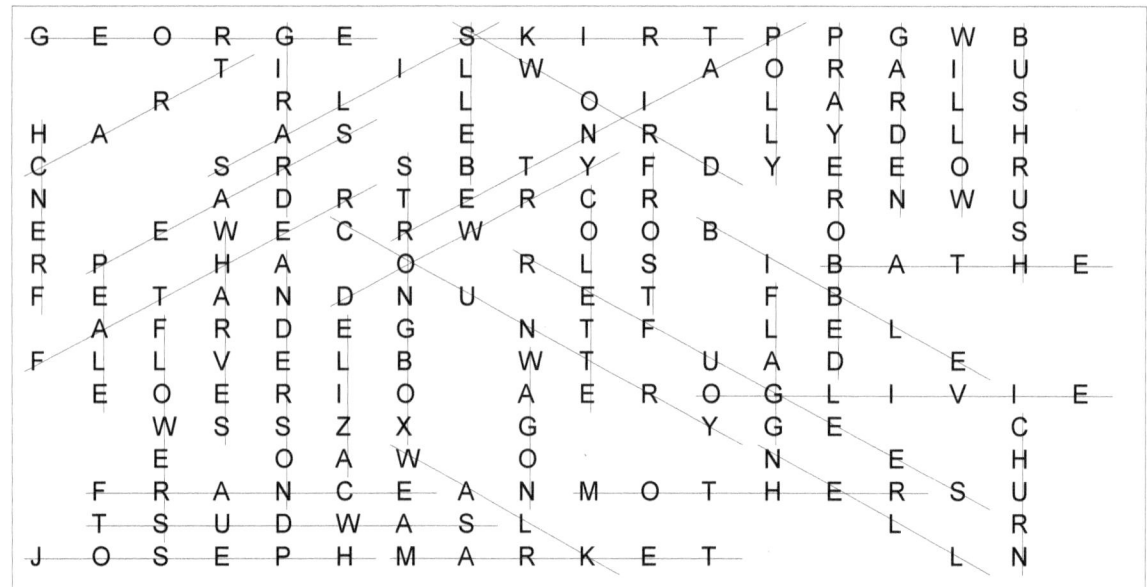

A man dumps Matilda's mother off of one. (4)
Author (8)
Chore to keep the children busy: ___ butter (5)
Coffeehouse partner with Matilda (5)
Country Matilda wants to go to (6)
Eliza's brother who lost his wife to yellow fever (6)
Eloped with her French tutor (7)
Family Matilda's mother hopes her daughter can marry into (7)
Girl who worked at the coffeehouse who dies of yellow fever (5)
Grandfather flirts with her as she nurses Matilda back to health. (5)
He believes black people can't catch yellow fever. (4)
He fell off a ladder and died of a broken neck. (6)
Hiding place for coffeehouse money (9)
It kills off the mosquitoes and the yellow fever. (5)
Joseph thinks Matilda should sell the coffeehouse so she has a nice ___. (5)
Matilda and her grandfather return to Philadelphia & discover they were ___. (6)
Matilda does this once a month and on special occasions. (5)
Matilda has to fight to get one said at her grandfather's funeral. (6)
Matilda is gathering these when she passes out, sick with the fever (5)
Matilda is taken to ___ Hill to recover from yellow fever. (4)
Matilda likes to read it at the end of each day. (5)

Matilda searches for this kind of a tree, knowing water will be nearby. (6)
Matilda stabs the robber with it. (5)
Matilda uses this to try to catch fish. (5)
Matilda's mother forbids her to go there for fear she might get sick. (7)
Nathaniel Benson throws these out a window at Matilda and Eliza. (7)
Nathaniel Benson's job (7)
Nathaniel sends Matilda a note saying he is safe at ___'s house. (5)
Parrot's name: King ___ (6)
People Matilda's grandfather thinks are to blame for the fever (8)
People mixed it with flour to make more bread. (7)
Place Matilda's grandfather wants her to get their food (6)
Place where people buy and sell food (6)
She is assumed dead but comes back to the coffeehouse at the end. (6)
Small child Matilda finds and cares for (4)
Stephen ___ turns Bush Hill into a safe hospital. (6)
The cat's name (5)
These doctors know how to treat the fever better than anyone else. (6)
These ring whenever someone dies. (5)
Transportation to the country (5)
Wealthy people flee there to escape the fever. (7)
What Matilda and Nathaniel do every evening (4)

Fever 1793 Crossword 1

Across
1. Matilda is taken to ___ Hill to recover from yellow fever.
2. Stephen ___ turns Bush Hill into a safe hospital.
4. Matilda is gathering these when she passes out, sick with the fever
7. Family whose farm Matilda's mother wants to send her to
8. Country Matilda wants to go to
9. Hiding place for coffeehouse money
15. Matilda has to fight to get one said at her grandfather's funeral.
17. Chore to keep the children busy: ___ butter
18. He fell off a ladder and died of a broken neck.
19. Matilda stabs the robber with it.
20. Place where people buy and sell food
21. Parrot's name: King ___

Down
1. These ring whenever someone dies.
3. Joseph thinks Matilda should sell the coffeehouse so she has a nice ___.
4. Nathaniel Benson's job
5. Author
6. The cat's name
10. He believes black people can't catch yellow fever.
11. Small child Matilda finds and cares for
12. Place the people at Bush Hill want Matilda to go to help out
13. Transportation to the country
14. People mixed it with flour to make more bread.
16. Coffeehouse partner with Matilda
17. A man dumps Matilda's mother off of one.
18. Grandfather flirts with her as she nurses Matilda back to health.

Fever 1793 Crossword 1 Answer Key

	1 B	U	S	H		2 G	I	R	A	R	D		4 P	E	5 A	R	6 S
	E										3 O		A		N		I
	7 L	U	D	I	N	G	T	O	N		W		I		D		L
	L								8 F	R	A	N	C	E			A
	9 S	10 T	R	11 O	N	12 G	B	O	X		Y		T		R		S
		U		E		R			13 W		E		S				
	14 S		S		L		15 P	R	A	Y	E	R		16 E		O	
	A		H		L		H		G			L		N			
	W						A		O			I					
	D		17 C	H	U	R	N		N			Z					
	U		A				A			18 F	A	T	H	E	R		
	19 S	W	O	R	D		G			L							
	T						E		20 M	A	R	K	E	T			
			T							G							
									21 G	E	O	R	G	E			

Across
1. Matilda is taken to ___ Hill to recover from yellow fever.
2. Stephen ___ turns Bush Hill into a safe hospital.
4. Matilda is gathering these when she passes out, sick with the fever
7. Family whose farm Matilda's mother wants to send her to
8. Country Matilda wants to go to
9. Hiding place for coffeehouse money
15. Matilda has to fight to get one said at her grandfather's funeral.
17. Chore to keep the children busy: ___ butter
18. He fell off a ladder and died of a broken neck.
19. Matilda stabs the robber with it.
20. Place where people buy and sell food
21. Parrot's name: King ___

Down
1. These ring whenever someone dies.
3. Joseph thinks Matilda should sell the coffeehouse so she has a nice ___.
4. Nathaniel Benson's job
5. Author
6. The cat's name
10. He believes black people can't catch yellow fever.
11. Small child Matilda finds and cares for
12. Place the people at Bush Hill want Matilda to go to help out
13. Transportation to the country
14. People mixed it with flour to make more bread.
16. Coffeehouse partner with Matilda
17. A man dumps Matilda's mother off of one.
18. Grandfather flirts with her as she nurses Matilda back to health.

Fever 1793 Crossword 2

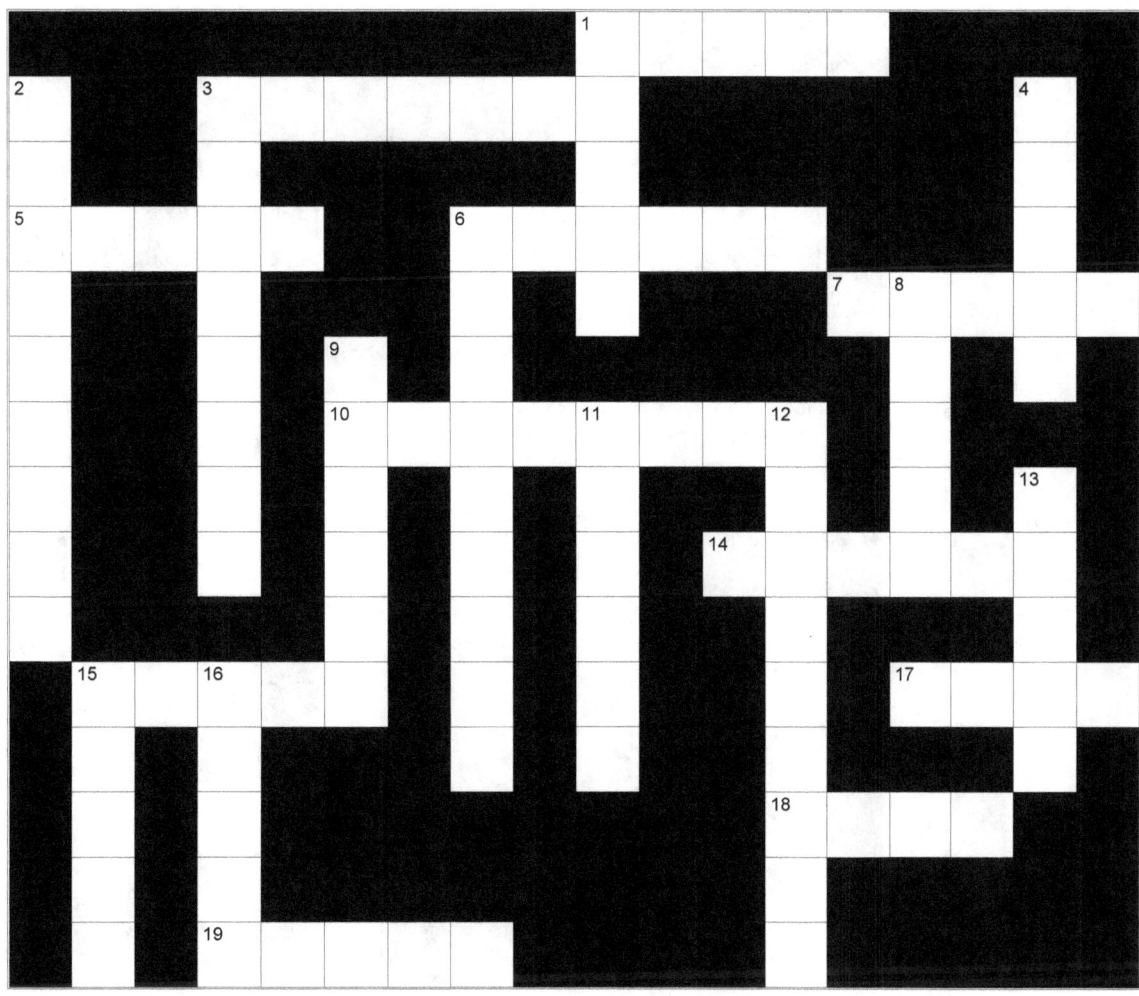

Across
1. Grandfather flirts with her as she nurses Matilda back to health.
3. Nathaniel Benson's job
5. Joseph thinks Matilda should sell the coffeehouse so she has a nice ___.
6. Eliza's brother who lost his wife to yellow fever
7. Matilda stabs the robber with it.
10. People Matilda's grandfather thinks are to blame for the fever
14. These doctors know how to treat the fever better than anyone else.
15. Matilda likes to read it at the end of each day.
17. A man dumps Matilda's mother off of one.
18. Matilda is taken to ___ Hill to recover from yellow fever.
19. Coffeehouse partner with Matilda

Down
1. It kills off the mosquitoes and the yellow fever.
2. Family whose farm Matilda's mother wants to send her to
3. Item Matilda buries with her grandfather
4. Matilda is gathering these when she passes out, sick with the fever
6. Matilda wants to get Thomas ___ to eat at the coffeehouse.
8. Transportation to the country
9. Country Matilda wants to go to
11. Stephen ___ turns Bush Hill into a safe hospital.
12. Hiding place for coffeehouse money
13. Chore to keep the children busy: ___ butter
15. These ring whenever someone dies.
16. Matilda does this once a month and on special occasions.

Fever 1793 Crossword 2 Answer Key

Across
1. Grandfather flirts with her as she nurses Matilda back to health.
3. Nathaniel Benson's job
5. Joseph thinks Matilda should sell the coffeehouse so she has a nice ___.
6. Eliza's brother who lost his wife to yellow fever
7. Matilda stabs the robber with it.
10. People Matilda's grandfather thinks are to blame for the fever
14. These doctors know how to treat the fever better than anyone else.
15. Matilda likes to read it at the end of each day.
17. A man dumps Matilda's mother off of one.
18. Matilda is taken to ___ Hill to recover from yellow fever.
19. Coffeehouse partner with Matilda

Down
1. It kills off the mosquitoes and the yellow fever.
2. Family whose farm Matilda's mother wants to send her to
3. Item Matilda buries with her grandfather
4. Matilda is gathering these when she passes out, sick with the fever
6. Matilda wants to get Thomas ___ to eat at the coffeehouse.
8. Transportation to the country
9. Country Matilda wants to go to
11. Stephen ___ turns Bush Hill into a safe hospital.
12. Hiding place for coffeehouse money
13. Chore to keep the children busy: ___ butter
15. These ring whenever someone dies.
16. Matilda does this once a month and on special occasions.

Fever 1793 Crossword 3

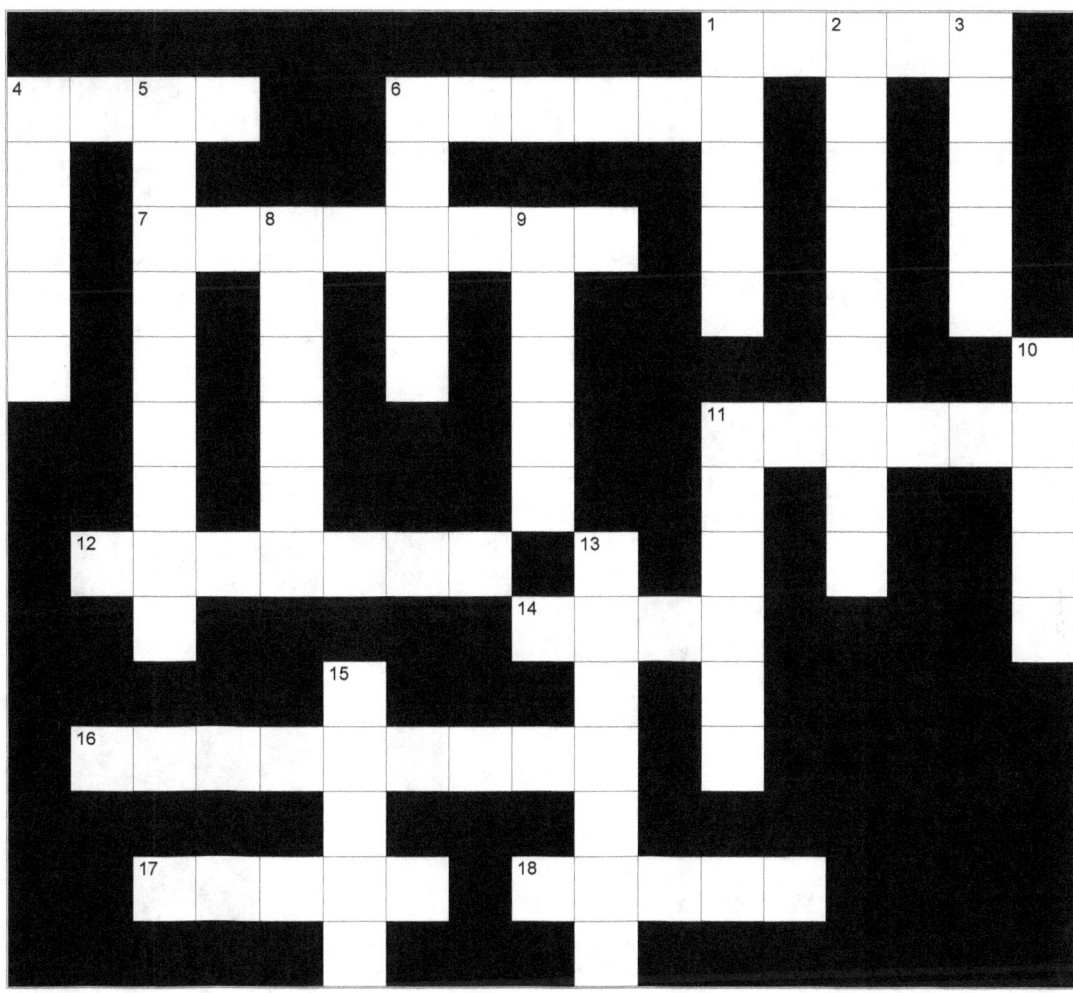

Across
1. The cat's name
4. Matilda is taken to ___ Hill to recover from yellow fever.
6. Matilda searches for this kind of a tree, knowing water will be nearby.
7. People Matilda's grandfather thinks are to blame for the fever
11. She is assumed dead but comes back to the coffeehouse at the end.
12. Eloped with her French tutor
14. What Matilda and Nathaniel do every evening
16. Matilda wants to get Thomas ___ to eat at the coffeehouse.
17. Joseph thinks Matilda should sell the coffeehouse so she has a nice ___.
18. Nathaniel sends Matilda a note saying he is safe at ___'s house.

Down
1. Matilda stabs the robber with it.
2. Family whose farm Matilda's mother wants to send her to
3. Matilda uses this to try to catch fish.
4. These ring whenever someone dies.
5. Hiding place for coffeehouse money
6. Transportation to the country
8. Country Matilda wants to go to
9. Coffeehouse partner with Matilda
10. It kills off the mosquitoes and the yellow fever.
11. Place where people buy and sell food
13. Nathaniel Benson's job
15. Matilda is gathering these when she passes out, sick with the fever

Fever 1793 Crossword 3 Answer Key

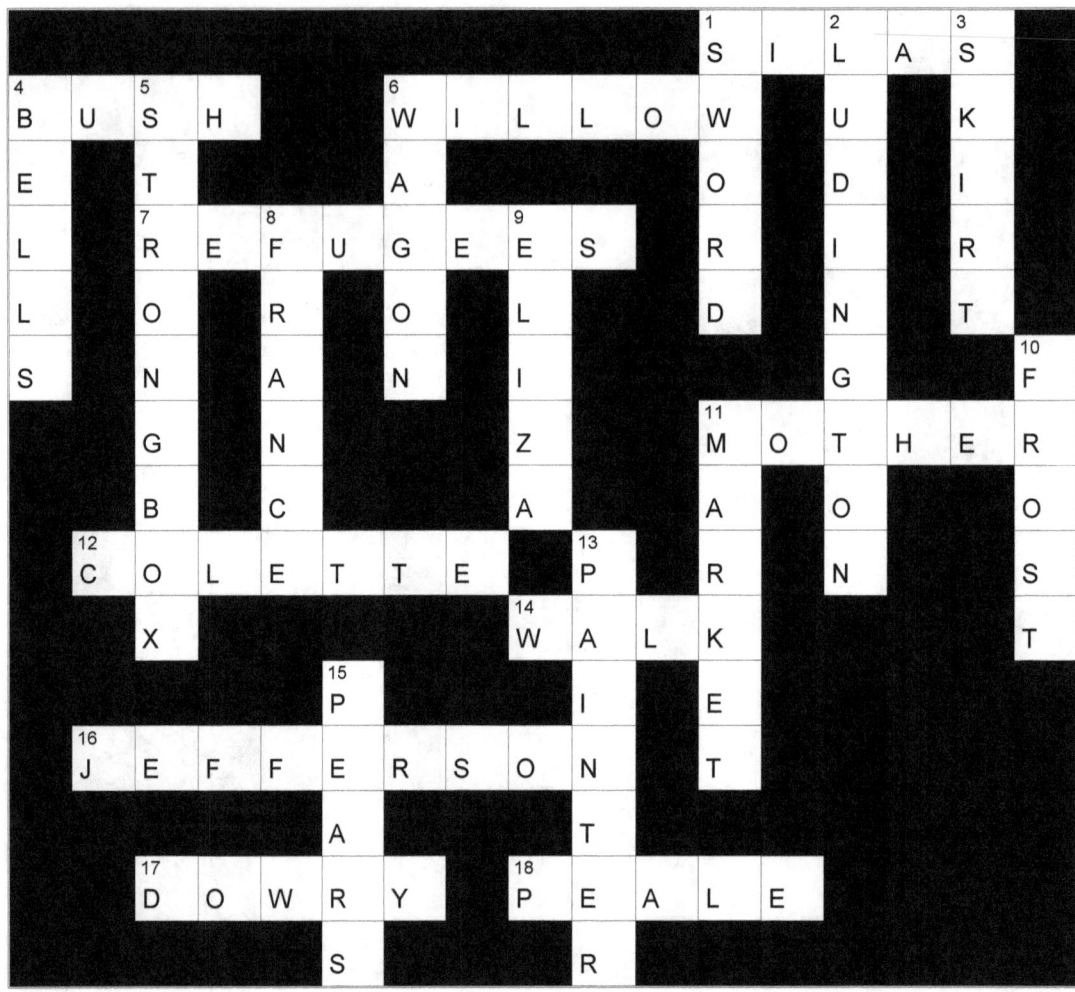

Across
1. The cat's name
4. Matilda is taken to ___ Hill to recover from yellow fever.
6. Matilda searches for this kind of a tree, knowing water will be nearby.
7. People Matilda's grandfather thinks are to blame for the fever
11. She is assumed dead but comes back to the coffeehouse at the end.
12. Eloped with her French tutor
14. What Matilda and Nathaniel do every evening
16. Matilda wants to get Thomas ___ to eat at the coffeehouse.
17. Joseph thinks Matilda should sell the coffeehouse so she has a nice ___.
18. Nathaniel sends Matilda a note saying he is safe at ___'s house.

Down
1. Matilda stabs the robber with it.
2. Family whose farm Matilda's mother wants to send her to
3. Matilda uses this to try to catch fish.
4. These ring whenever someone dies.
5. Hiding place for coffeehouse money
6. Transportation to the country
8. Country Matilda wants to go to
9. Coffeehouse partner with Matilda
10. It kills off the mosquitoes and the yellow fever.
11. Place where people buy and sell food
13. Nathaniel Benson's job
15. Matilda is gathering these when she passes out, sick with the fever

Fever 1793 Crossword 4

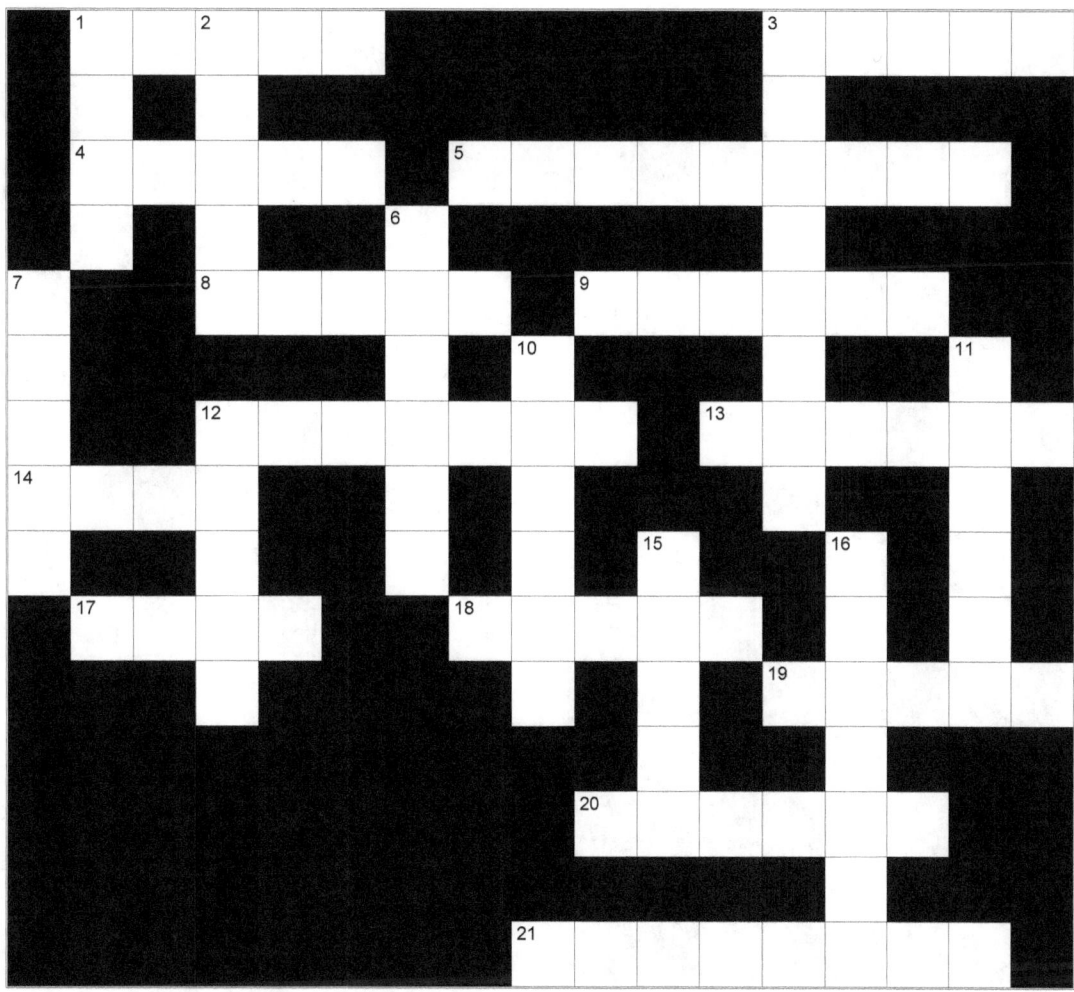

Across
1. Matilda likes to read it at the end of each day.
3. Matilda is gathering these when she passes out, sick with the fever
4. The cat's name
5. Matilda wants to get Thomas ___ to eat at the coffeehouse.
8. Matilda uses this to try to catch fish.
9. Parrot's name: King ___
12. Wealthy people flee there to escape the fever.
13. Matilda searches for this kind of a tree, knowing water will be nearby.
14. He believes black people can't catch yellow fever.
17. A man dumps Matilda's mother off of one.
18. Nathaniel sends Matilda a note saying he is safe at ___'s house.
19. Joseph thinks Matilda should sell the coffeehouse so she has a nice ___.
20. He fell off a ladder and died of a broken neck.
21. Author

Down
1. Matilda is taken to ___ Hill to recover from yellow fever.
2. These ring whenever someone dies.
3. Item Matilda buries with her grandfather
6. Country Matilda wants to go to
7. Matilda stabs the robber with it.
10. Matilda has to fight to get one said at her grandfather's funeral.
11. She is assumed dead but comes back to the coffeehouse at the end.
12. Chore to keep the children busy: ___ butter
15. Coffeehouse partner with Matilda
16. Nathaniel Benson throws these out a window at Matilda and Eliza.

Fever 1793 Crossword 4 Answer Key

Across
1. Matilda likes to read it at the end of each day.
3. Matilda is gathering these when she passes out, sick with the fever
4. The cat's name
5. Matilda wants to get Thomas ___ to eat at the coffeehouse.
8. Matilda uses this to try to catch fish.
9. Parrot's name: King ___
12. Wealthy people flee there to escape the fever.
13. Matilda searches for this kind of a tree, knowing water will be nearby.
14. He believes black people can't catch yellow fever.
17. A man dumps Matilda's mother off of one.
18. Nathaniel sends Matilda a note saying he is safe at ___'s house.
19. Joseph thinks Matilda should sell the coffeehouse so she has a nice ___.
20. He fell off a ladder and died of a broken neck.
21. Author

Down
1. Matilda is taken to ___ Hill to recover from yellow fever.
2. These ring whenever someone dies.
3. Item Matilda buries with her grandfather
6. Country Matilda wants to go to
7. Matilda stabs the robber with it.
10. Matilda has to fight to get one said at her grandfather's funeral.
11. She is assumed dead but comes back to the coffeehouse at the end.
12. Chore to keep the children busy: ___ butter
15. Coffeehouse partner with Matilda
16. Nathaniel Benson throws these out a window at Matilda and Eliza.

Fever 1793

ANDERSON	FRENCH	BELLS	GIRARD	FATHER
SILAS	WHARVES	WASHINGTON	STRONGBOX	NELL
REFUGEES	GARDEN	FREE SPACE	JOSEPH	FROST
CART	MARKET	COLETTE	FLOWERS	ORPHANAGE
GEORGE	PEALE	SWORD	POLLY	DOWRY

Fever 1793

BUSH	PRAYER	WILLOW	FRANCE	WALK
SKIRT	OGLIVIE	PAINTER	RUSH	COUNTRY
MOTHER	BIBLE	FREE SPACE	ELIZA	JEFFERSON
PEARS	PORTRAIT	FLAGG	BATHE	WAGON
LUDINGTON	SAWDUST	DOWRY	POLLY	SWORD

Fever 1793

ANDERSON	WHARVES	GEORGE	FATHER	FRANCE
POLLY	FLAGG	STRONGBOX	SILAS	PEARS
CART	REFUGEES	FREE SPACE	COUNTRY	WAGON
WILLOW	BUSH	FROST	OGLIVIE	MARKET
JOSEPH	SAWDUST	BIBLE	BATHE	PRAYER

Fever 1793

MOTHER	PAINTER	LUDINGTON	WASHINGTON	SWORD
RUSH	GIRARD	ELIZA	GARDEN	CHURN
PEALE	JEFFERSON	FREE SPACE	SKIRT	ROBBED
FLOWERS	BELLS	DOWRY	PORTRAIT	COLETTE
ORPHANAGE	WALK	PRAYER	BATHE	BIBLE

Fever 1793

GIRARD	MOTHER	COUNTRY	DOWRY	ELIZA
PRAYER	CART	FRANCE	BELLS	PEARS
WHARVES	FROST	FREE SPACE	RUSH	PORTRAIT
SILAS	SWORD	CHURN	FRENCH	WALK
WILLOW	GEORGE	SAWDUST	STRONGBOX	JOSEPH

Fever 1793

FLOWERS	MARKET	PAINTER	FATHER	COLETTE
SKIRT	FLAGG	ORPHANAGE	BIBLE	ANDERSON
GARDEN	POLLY	FREE SPACE	OGLIVIE	JEFFERSON
ROBBED	LUDINGTON	NELL	WAGON	PEALE
BUSH	WASHINGTON	JOSEPH	STRONGBOX	SAWDUST

Fever 1793

FRANCE	GARDEN	LUDINGTON	BATHE	ELIZA
SKIRT	ANDERSON	BELLS	PEALE	NELL
CART	WILLOW	FREE SPACE	SWORD	FROST
ORPHANAGE	MARKET	GIRARD	WASHINGTON	SAWDUST
PAINTER	DOWRY	WAGON	JEFFERSON	POLLY

Fever 1793

COUNTRY	PORTRAIT	MOTHER	COLETTE	OGLIVIE
REFUGEES	RUSH	FLAGG	WALK	GEORGE
FRENCH	CHURN	FREE SPACE	FLOWERS	ROBBED
FATHER	BIBLE	WHARVES	BUSH	PEARS
PRAYER	SILAS	POLLY	JEFFERSON	WAGON

Fever 1793

GEORGE	FRENCH	ROBBED	FLOWERS	WASHINGTON
ORPHANAGE	BELLS	BIBLE	WAGON	PEARS
JOSEPH	BATHE	FREE SPACE	WILLOW	POLLY
SWORD	PRAYER	REFUGEES	RUSH	NELL
GARDEN	WHARVES	ANDERSON	PEALE	COUNTRY

Fever 1793

FLAGG	FATHER	WALK	FRANCE	PAINTER
LUDINGTON	GIRARD	CHURN	FROST	ELIZA
MARKET	SKIRT	FREE SPACE	OGLIVIE	JEFFERSON
DOWRY	STRONGBOX	MOTHER	PORTRAIT	COLETTE
CART	SAWDUST	COUNTRY	PEALE	ANDERSON

Fever 1793

JOSEPH	CART	WALK	DOWRY	PAINTER
MARKET	WAGON	SAWDUST	OGLIVIE	NELL
JEFFERSON	FLAGG	FREE SPACE	PRAYER	WILLOW
BELLS	WHARVES	FROST	ELIZA	COLETTE
FLOWERS	BATHE	SWORD	SILAS	MOTHER

Fever 1793

POLLY	FRENCH	SKIRT	FRANCE	ANDERSON
BIBLE	LUDINGTON	ROBBED	RUSH	STRONGBOX
GARDEN	PEALE	FREE SPACE	PEARS	REFUGEES
PORTRAIT	GEORGE	WASHINGTON	FATHER	GIRARD
COUNTRY	ORPHANAGE	MOTHER	SILAS	SWORD

Fever 1793

LUDINGTON	SWORD	RUSH	MOTHER	ANDERSON
BIBLE	FROST	WILLOW	ROBBED	WHARVES
FATHER	GIRARD	FREE SPACE	SKIRT	FRANCE
ELIZA	COUNTRY	OGLIVIE	PEARS	FLAGG
CART	CHURN	WASHINGTON	REFUGEES	PAINTER

Fever 1793

SAWDUST	NELL	BUSH	BELLS	PEALE
WAGON	SILAS	GARDEN	BATHE	POLLY
FLOWERS	WALK	FREE SPACE	DOWRY	PRAYER
JEFFERSON	ORPHANAGE	JOSEPH	MARKET	GEORGE
PORTRAIT	FRENCH	PAINTER	REFUGEES	WASHINGTON

Fever 1793

FLOWERS	COLETTE	GARDEN	PRAYER	JOSEPH
NELL	STRONGBOX	DOWRY	PEARS	CART
SKIRT	WASHINGTON	FREE SPACE	ROBBED	FROST
FRANCE	GIRARD	SILAS	COUNTRY	SAWDUST
MOTHER	WALK	GEORGE	PORTRAIT	WHARVES

Fever 1793

MARKET	SWORD	BIBLE	POLLY	ORPHANAGE
FRENCH	ELIZA	ANDERSON	RUSH	BUSH
JEFFERSON	PAINTER	FREE SPACE	FLAGG	OGLIVIE
REFUGEES	WILLOW	BELLS	CHURN	PEALE
FATHER	WAGON	WHARVES	PORTRAIT	GEORGE

Fever 1793

WAGON	GEORGE	CART	BELLS	GARDEN
FLOWERS	POLLY	PORTRAIT	PAINTER	WASHINGTON
BATHE	GIRARD	FREE SPACE	NELL	JOSEPH
FATHER	CHURN	WALK	ORPHANAGE	COLETTE
FLAGG	ANDERSON	STRONGBOX	SILAS	JEFFERSON

Fever 1793

BIBLE	PEALE	WHARVES	DOWRY	WILLOW
MOTHER	LUDINGTON	SAWDUST	BUSH	COUNTRY
RUSH	FRENCH	FREE SPACE	PEARS	FROST
FRANCE	ROBBED	MARKET	OGLIVIE	ELIZA
REFUGEES	SKIRT	JEFFERSON	SILAS	STRONGBOX

Fever 1793

FLOWERS	ROBBED	ELIZA	PORTRAIT	JOSEPH
WASHINGTON	COLETTE	CART	OGLIVIE	PAINTER
REFUGEES	BUSH	FREE SPACE	WHARVES	WALK
FROST	JEFFERSON	NELL	PRAYER	SAWDUST
FRENCH	FLAGG	MOTHER	BELLS	ANDERSON

Fever 1793

LUDINGTON	WILLOW	SWORD	SILAS	BIBLE
POLLY	GIRARD	STRONGBOX	MARKET	DOWRY
CHURN	PEARS	FREE SPACE	RUSH	COUNTRY
PEALE	GEORGE	FRANCE	ORPHANAGE	SKIRT
WAGON	BATHE	ANDERSON	BELLS	MOTHER

Fever 1793

STRONGBOX	SKIRT	CART	GIRARD	ANDERSON
COUNTRY	WASHINGTON	BIBLE	PAINTER	SAWDUST
JOSEPH	FLOWERS	FREE SPACE	FROST	JEFFERSON
POLLY	SILAS	SWORD	RUSH	PEALE
GEORGE	WILLOW	LUDINGTON	WALK	FATHER

Fever 1793

FLAGG	FRENCH	ORPHANAGE	PEARS	NELL
WHARVES	FRANCE	ELIZA	BUSH	MOTHER
ROBBED	MARKET	FREE SPACE	REFUGEES	BATHE
WAGON	PRAYER	GARDEN	DOWRY	COLETTE
BELLS	PORTRAIT	FATHER	WALK	LUDINGTON

Fever 1793

FRENCH	POLLY	FRANCE	REFUGEES	WAGON
ANDERSON	JOSEPH	SWORD	COLETTE	GIRARD
FLAGG	PEALE	FREE SPACE	WALK	FROST
GARDEN	BATHE	BIBLE	LUDINGTON	WHARVES
CART	ORPHANAGE	DOWRY	FATHER	COUNTRY

Fever 1793

RUSH	SKIRT	STRONGBOX	WILLOW	SAWDUST
BUSH	BELLS	JEFFERSON	ELIZA	PRAYER
PEARS	NELL	FREE SPACE	FLOWERS	MARKET
CHURN	GEORGE	MOTHER	ROBBED	PORTRAIT
SILAS	PAINTER	COUNTRY	FATHER	DOWRY

Fever 1793

POLLY	CHURN	FRENCH	GARDEN	REFUGEES
BIBLE	BELLS	FRANCE	GIRARD	ROBBED
RUSH	WILLOW	FREE SPACE	SAWDUST	PAINTER
CART	PORTRAIT	SKIRT	PEALE	FROST
PRAYER	WAGON	PEARS	SILAS	ORPHANAGE

Fever 1793

JOSEPH	DOWRY	MOTHER	WALK	FLAGG
FATHER	COLETTE	ANDERSON	NELL	SWORD
MARKET	BATHE	FREE SPACE	ELIZA	COUNTRY
FLOWERS	WASHINGTON	GEORGE	LUDINGTON	WHARVES
JEFFERSON	OGLIVIE	ORPHANAGE	SILAS	PEARS

Fever 1793

GARDEN	MARKET	FLAGG	PEARS	REFUGEES
SKIRT	FLOWERS	WHARVES	ELIZA	ORPHANAGE
BIBLE	DOWRY	FREE SPACE	ANDERSON	BATHE
WILLOW	POLLY	JOSEPH	FROST	FRANCE
COUNTRY	CHURN	OGLIVIE	ROBBED	CART

Fever 1793

BELLS	SILAS	SWORD	NELL	FRENCH
PRAYER	PAINTER	LUDINGTON	GIRARD	GEORGE
WALK	SAWDUST	FREE SPACE	FATHER	WASHINGTON
BUSH	WAGON	PORTRAIT	COLETTE	STRONGBOX
PEALE	MOTHER	CART	ROBBED	OGLIVIE

Fever 1793

FROST	SKIRT	SILAS	FLOWERS	FATHER
FLAGG	GARDEN	ELIZA	REFUGEES	NELL
SAWDUST	ORPHANAGE	FREE SPACE	STRONGBOX	MARKET
DOWRY	SWORD	JOSEPH	COUNTRY	LUDINGTON
MOTHER	ROBBED	GEORGE	BUSH	FRANCE

Fever 1793

WALK	BELLS	PAINTER	WASHINGTON	PRAYER
JEFFERSON	ANDERSON	POLLY	COLETTE	WAGON
WILLOW	BATHE	FREE SPACE	BIBLE	CART
CHURN	PEALE	WHARVES	GIRARD	PORTRAIT
OGLIVIE	RUSH	FRANCE	BUSH	GEORGE

Fever 1793

SKIRT	REFUGEES	BELLS	POLLY	MOTHER
WHARVES	LUDINGTON	FROST	JOSEPH	PRAYER
GARDEN	FATHER	FREE SPACE	PAINTER	PEARS
ROBBED	GEORGE	BUSH	DOWRY	OGLIVIE
WILLOW	MARKET	SILAS	COUNTRY	SAWDUST

Fever 1793

BIBLE	CART	FRANCE	COLETTE	WAGON
ELIZA	SWORD	JEFFERSON	WALK	FRENCH
NELL	FLOWERS	FREE SPACE	PEALE	FLAGG
RUSH	GIRARD	CHURN	BATHE	ORPHANAGE
ANDERSON	WASHINGTON	SAWDUST	COUNTRY	SILAS

Fever 1793 Vocabulary Word List

No.	Word	Clue/Definition
1.	ABHORRED	Detested utterly; loathed; hated
2.	ABIDE	Tolerate; put up with; stay
3.	AILS	Causes physical or emotional pain
4.	BEGRUDGE	Envy or resent the good fortune of someone else
5.	BESTIR	Stir up; rouse; bring to action
6.	BILIOUS	Extremely unpleasant or distasteful in regards to sickness
7.	BRANDISH	Shake or wave a weapon
8.	BUNKUM	Insincere or ridiculous talk
9.	CACKLED	Voiced a shrill, broken laugh
10.	CAJOLING	Persuading with flattery or promises
11.	COMMOTION	Disturbance; chaotic activity
12.	CONCEDED	Yielded; admitted; relinquished; reluctantly acknowledged
13.	DEMURE	Shy; modest; coy
14.	DESTITUTE	Lacking food, clothing, and shelter; without necessities
15.	DIM	Not bright; dull
16.	DISENTANGLING	Unravelling; becoming free from
17.	DROLL	Amusing or funny in an odd or dry way
18.	EXORBITANT	Excessive; extreme; unreasonable
19.	EXTINGUISH	Put out or bring to an end
20.	FAMISHED	Extremely hungry
21.	FATIGUE	Weariness from bodily or mental exhaustion
22.	FETID	Having an offensive odor
23.	FORGE	Workshop of a blacksmith
24.	GAUNT	Extremely thin and bony
25.	GUMPTION	Aggressiveness; boldness
26.	HARRUMPHED	Offered brief, critical comments
27.	HASTE	Swiftness of motion; hurry; rush
28.	HOISTED	Lifted; raised up
29.	IMPLORE	Beg urgently
30.	IMPUDENCE	Quality of being offensively bold; nerve; rudeness
31.	INSTILL	Gradually put something into someone's mind or feelings
32.	INVALID	Someone too weak to care for himself
33.	JAUNDICED	Having a yellow discoloration of the skin due to disease
34.	LOITERING	Lingering aimlessly; hanging about with no purpose
35.	MELODIOUS	Sweet-sounding
36.	MIASMA	Poisonous fumes or germs polluting the atmosphere
37.	PESTILENCE	A deadly disease
38.	PLACID	Quiet; calm; peaceful
39.	PROPRIETOR	Owner of a business establishment
40.	PURGE	Cleanse; purify
41.	PUTRID	Rotten; decaying
42.	RELENT	Slacken; abandon; withdraw; give in
43.	RESOLUTELY	Firmly determined
44.	RUCKUS	Noisy commotion or disturbance
45.	SALVAGE	Save; rescue
46.	SCURRILOUS	Obscene; vulgar; abusive
47.	SHROUD	Cloth or sheet wrapping a corpse
48.	SNIPPET	Small or insignificant person
49.	SOLEMN	Serious; not to be taken lightly
50.	SOLITARY	Alone or unattended
51.	TAUT	Tightly drawn; tense

Copyrighted

Fever 1793 Vocabulary Word List Continued

No.	Word	Clue/Definition
52.	TETHERED	Attached by a short rope
53.	TRIFLING	Small; of little importance
54.	TRUNDLED	Moved along
55.	VANITY	Excessive pride in one's appearance
56.	VEHEMENTLY	With great passion or energy
57.	VENTURING	Taking a risk or braving dangers
58.	VICTUALS	Food fit for humans to eat
59.	WEARILY	In a fatigued, tired, or worn-out way
60.	WHARVES	Landing places where ships may tie up to load or unload

Fever 1793 Vocabulary Fill In The Blanks 1

1. Detested utterly; loathed; hated
2. Having a yellow discoloration of the skin due to disease
3. Lingering aimlessly; hanging about with no purpose
4. Save; rescue
5. Cloth or sheet wrapping a corpse
6. Gradually put something into someone's mind or feelings
7. Rotten; decaying
8. Envy or resent the good fortune of someone else
9. Tolerate; put up with; stay
10. Disturbance; chaotic activity
11. Put out or bring to an end
12. Small or insignificant person
13. Noisy commotion or disturbance
14. Sweet-sounding
15. Obscene; vulgar; abusive
16. Slacken; abandon; withdraw; give in
17. Aggressiveness; boldness
18. Extremely hungry
19. Persuading with flattery or promises
20. Firmly determined

Fever 1793 Vocabulary Fill In The Blanks 1 Answer Key

ABHORRED	1. Detested utterly; loathed; hated
JAUNDICED	2. Having a yellow discoloration of the skin due to disease
LOITERING	3. Lingering aimlessly; hanging about with no purpose
SALVAGE	4. Save; rescue
SHROUD	5. Cloth or sheet wrapping a corpse
INSTILL	6. Gradually put something into someone's mind or feelings
PUTRID	7. Rotten; decaying
BEGRUDGE	8. Envy or resent the good fortune of someone else
ABIDE	9. Tolerate; put up with; stay
COMMOTION	10. Disturbance; chaotic activity
EXTINGUISH	11. Put out or bring to an end
SNIPPET	12. Small or insignificant person
RUCKUS	13. Noisy commotion or disturbance
MELODIOUS	14. Sweet-sounding
SCURRILOUS	15. Obscene; vulgar; abusive
RELENT	16. Slacken; abandon; withdraw; give in
GUMPTION	17. Aggressiveness; boldness
FAMISHED	18. Extremely hungry
CAJOLING	19. Persuading with flattery or promises
RESOLUTELY	20. Firmly determined

Fever 1793 Vocabulary Fill In The Blanks 2

1. With great passion or energy
2. Envy or resent the good fortune of someone else
3. Lifted; raised up
4. Rotten; decaying
5. Quiet; calm; peaceful
6. Put out or bring to an end
7. Having a yellow discoloration of the skin due to disease
8. Shy; modest; coy
9. Landing places where ships may tie up to load or unload
10. Stir up; rouse; bring to action
11. Moved along
12. Owner of a business establishment
13. Gradually put something into someone's mind or feelings
14. Amusing or funny in an odd or dry way
15. Weariness from bodily or mental exhaustion
16. Cloth or sheet wrapping a corpse
17. Tightly drawn; tense
18. Serious; not to be taken lightly
19. Extremely hungry
20. Offered brief, critical comments

Fever 1793 Vocabulary Fill In The Blanks 2 Answer Key

VEHEMENTLY	1. With great passion or energy
BEGRUDGE	2. Envy or resent the good fortune of someone else
HOISTED	3. Lifted; raised up
PUTRID	4. Rotten; decaying
PLACID	5. Quiet; calm; peaceful
EXTINGUISH	6. Put out or bring to an end
JAUNDICED	7. Having a yellow discoloration of the skin due to disease
DEMURE	8. Shy; modest; coy
WHARVES	9. Landing places where ships may tie up to load or unload
BESTIR	10. Stir up; rouse; bring to action
TRUNDLED	11. Moved along
PROPRIETOR	12. Owner of a business establishment
INSTILL	13. Gradually put something into someone's mind or feelings
DROLL	14. Amusing or funny in an odd or dry way
FATIGUE	15. Weariness from bodily or mental exhaustion
SHROUD	16. Cloth or sheet wrapping a corpse
TAUT	17. Tightly drawn; tense
SOLEMN	18. Serious; not to be taken lightly
FAMISHED	19. Extremely hungry
HARRUMPHED	20. Offered brief, critical comments

Copyrighted

Fever 1793 Vocabulary Fill In The Blanks 3

_____ 1. In a fatigued, tired, or worn-out way

_____ 2. Noisy commotion or disturbance

_____ 3. Detested utterly; loathed; hated

_____ 4. Obscene; vulgar; abusive

_____ 5. Causes physical or emotional pain

_____ 6. Gradually put something into someone's mind or feelings

_____ 7. Excessive pride in one's appearance

_____ 8. Taking a risk or braving dangers

_____ 9. Lingering aimlessly; hanging about with no purpose

_____ 10. Having a yellow discoloration of the skin due to disease

_____ 11. Insincere or ridiculous talk

_____ 12. Quality of being offensively bold; nerve; rudeness

_____ 13. Persuading with flattery or promises

_____ 14. Rotten; decaying

_____ 15. Firmly determined

_____ 16. Extremely unpleasant or distasteful in regards to sickness

_____ 17. Sweet-sounding

_____ 18. Workshop of a blacksmith

_____ 19. Someone too weak to care for himself

_____ 20. Attached by a short rope

Fever 1793 Vocabulary Fill In The Blanks 3 Answer Key

WEARILY	1. In a fatigued, tired, or worn-out way
RUCKUS	2. Noisy commotion or disturbance
ABHORRED	3. Detested utterly; loathed; hated
SCURRILOUS	4. Obscene; vulgar; abusive
AILS	5. Causes physical or emotional pain
INSTILL	6. Gradually put something into someone's mind or feelings
VANITY	7. Excessive pride in one's appearance
VENTURING	8. Taking a risk or braving dangers
LOITERING	9. Lingering aimlessly; hanging about with no purpose
JAUNDICED	10. Having a yellow discoloration of the skin due to disease
BUNKUM	11. Insincere or ridiculous talk
IMPUDENCE	12. Quality of being offensively bold; nerve; rudeness
CAJOLING	13. Persuading with flattery or promises
PUTRID	14. Rotten; decaying
RESOLUTELY	15. Firmly determined
BILIOUS	16. Extremely unpleasant or distasteful in regards to sickness
MELODIOUS	17. Sweet-sounding
FORGE	18. Workshop of a blacksmith
INVALID	19. Someone too weak to care for himself
TETHERED	20. Attached by a short rope

Fever 1793 Vocabulary Fill In The Blanks 4

_____ 1. Extremely hungry

_____ 2. Swiftness of motion; hurry; rush

_____ 3. Serious; not to be taken lightly

_____ 4. Beg urgently

_____ 5. Landing places where ships may tie up to load or unload

_____ 6. Poisonous fumes or germs polluting the atmosphere

_____ 7. Voiced a shrill, broken laugh

_____ 8. Excessive; extreme; unreasonable

_____ 9. Yielded; admitted; relinquished; reluctantly acknowledged

_____ 10. Amusing or funny in an odd or dry way

_____ 11. Small or insignificant person

_____ 12. Extremely thin and bony

_____ 13. Small; of little importance

_____ 14. Weariness from bodily or mental exhaustion

_____ 15. Sweet-sounding

_____ 16. Excessive pride in one's appearance

_____ 17. Disturbance; chaotic activity

_____ 18. Offered brief, critical comments

_____ 19. Obscene; vulgar; abusive

_____ 20. Causes physical or emotional pain

Fever 1793 Vocabulary Fill In The Blanks 4 Answer Key

FAMISHED	1. Extremely hungry
HASTE	2. Swiftness of motion; hurry; rush
SOLEMN	3. Serious; not to be taken lightly
IMPLORE	4. Beg urgently
WHARVES	5. Landing places where ships may tie up to load or unload
MIASMA	6. Poisonous fumes or germs polluting the atmosphere
CACKLED	7. Voiced a shrill, broken laugh
EXORBITANT	8. Excessive; extreme; unreasonable
CONCEDED	9. Yielded; admitted; relinquished; reluctantly acknowledged
DROLL	10. Amusing or funny in an odd or dry way
SNIPPET	11. Small or insignificant person
GAUNT	12. Extremely thin and bony
TRIFLING	13. Small; of little importance
FATIGUE	14. Weariness from bodily or mental exhaustion
MELODIOUS	15. Sweet-sounding
VANITY	16. Excessive pride in one's appearance
COMMOTION	17. Disturbance; chaotic activity
HARRUMPHED	18. Offered brief, critical comments
SCURRILOUS	19. Obscene; vulgar; abusive
AILS	20. Causes physical or emotional pain

Fever 1793 Vocabulary Matching 1

___ 1. SOLITARY   A. Gradually put something into someone's mind or feelings
___ 2. DESTITUTE   B. Shake or wave a weapon
___ 3. CONCEDED   C. Aggressiveness; boldness
___ 4. MELODIOUS   D. With great passion or energy
___ 5. GUMPTION   E. Quiet; calm; peaceful
___ 6. DISENTANGLING F. Unravelling; becoming free from
___ 7. IMPUDENCE   G. Lacking food, clothing, and shelter; without necessities
___ 8. BRANDISH   H. Sweet-sounding
___ 9. GAUNT   I. Save; rescue
___10. EXTINGUISH   J. Alone or unattended
___11. INSTILL   K. Extremely thin and bony
___12. INVALID   L. Put out or bring to an end
___13. ABHORRED   M. Offered brief, critical comments
___14. VEHEMENTLY   N. Landing places where ships may tie up to load or unload
___15. PLACID   O. Someone too weak to care for himself
___16. HARRUMPHED   P. Firmly determined
___17. FATIGUE   Q. Attached by a short rope
___18. WHARVES   R. Quality of being offensively bold; nerve; rudeness
___19. RESOLUTELY   S. Yielded; admitted; relinquished; reluctantly acknowledged
___20. SOLEMN   T. Serious; not to be taken lightly
___21. BESTIR   U. Amusing or funny in an odd or dry way
___22. SCURRILOUS   V. Obscene; vulgar; abusive
___23. SALVAGE   W. Weariness from bodily or mental exhaustion
___24. TETHERED   X. Detested utterly; loathed; hated
___25. DROLL   Y. Stir up; rouse; bring to action

Fever 1793 Vocabulary Matching 1 Answer Key

J - 1.	SOLITARY	A. Gradually put something into someone's mind or feelings
G - 2.	DESTITUTE	B. Shake or wave a weapon
S - 3.	CONCEDED	C. Aggressiveness; boldness
H - 4.	MELODIOUS	D. With great passion or energy
C - 5.	GUMPTION	E. Quiet; calm; peaceful
F - 6.	DISENTANGLING	F. Unravelling; becoming free from
R - 7.	IMPUDENCE	G. Lacking food, clothing, and shelter; without necessities
B - 8.	BRANDISH	H. Sweet-sounding
K - 9.	GAUNT	I. Save; rescue
L - 10.	EXTINGUISH	J. Alone or unattended
A - 11.	INSTILL	K. Extremely thin and bony
O - 12.	INVALID	L. Put out or bring to an end
X - 13.	ABHORRED	M. Offered brief, critical comments
D - 14.	VEHEMENTLY	N. Landing places where ships may tie up to load or unload
E - 15.	PLACID	O. Someone too weak to care for himself
M - 16.	HARRUMPHED	P. Firmly determined
W - 17.	FATIGUE	Q. Attached by a short rope
N - 18.	WHARVES	R. Quality of being offensively bold; nerve; rudeness
P - 19.	RESOLUTELY	S. Yielded; admitted; relinquished; reluctantly acknowledged
T - 20.	SOLEMN	T. Serious; not to be taken lightly
Y - 21.	BESTIR	U. Amusing or funny in an odd or dry way
V - 22.	SCURRILOUS	V. Obscene; vulgar; abusive
I - 23.	SALVAGE	W. Weariness from bodily or mental exhaustion
Q - 24.	TETHERED	X. Detested utterly; loathed; hated
U - 25.	DROLL	Y. Stir up; rouse; bring to action

Fever 1793 Vocabulary Matching 2

___ 1. RUCKUS	A. Extremely thin and bony
___ 2. SCURRILOUS	B. Unravelling; becoming free from
___ 3. TAUT	C. Extremely hungry
___ 4. PUTRID	D. Cloth or sheet wrapping a corpse
___ 5. CACKLED	E. Weariness from bodily or mental exhaustion
___ 6. FATIGUE	F. Poisonous fumes or germs polluting the atmosphere
___ 7. HASTE	G. Swiftness of motion; hurry; rush
___ 8. GAUNT	H. Lingering aimlessly; hanging about with no purpose
___ 9. MIASMA	I. Moved along
___10. SHROUD	J. Voiced a shrill, broken laugh
___11. TRUNDLED	K. Excessive pride in one's appearance
___12. FETID	L. Taking a risk or braving dangers
___13. ABHORRED	M. Tightly drawn; tense
___14. FORGE	N. Obscene; vulgar; abusive
___15. AILS	O. In a fatigued, tired, or worn-out way
___16. WEARILY	P. Causes physical or emotional pain
___17. WHARVES	Q. Landing places where ships may tie up to load or unload
___18. VENTURING	R. Workshop of a blacksmith
___19. VEHEMENTLY	S. With great passion or energy
___20. TRIFLING	T. Extremely unpleasant or distasteful in regards to sickness
___21. DISENTANGLING	U. Detested utterly; loathed; hated
___22. LOITERING	V. Having an offensive odor
___23. FAMISHED	W. Noisy commotion or disturbance
___24. BILIOUS	X. Rotten; decaying
___25. VANITY	Y. Small; of little importance

Fever 1793 Vocabulary Matching 2 Answer Key

W -	1. RUCKUS	A.	Extremely thin and bony
N -	2. SCURRILOUS	B.	Unravelling; becoming free from
M -	3. TAUT	C.	Extremely hungry
X -	4. PUTRID	D.	Cloth or sheet wrapping a corpse
J -	5. CACKLED	E.	Weariness from bodily or mental exhaustion
E -	6. FATIGUE	F.	Poisonous fumes or germs polluting the atmosphere
G -	7. HASTE	G.	Swiftness of motion; hurry; rush
A -	8. GAUNT	H.	Lingering aimlessly; hanging about with no purpose
F -	9. MIASMA	I.	Moved along
D -	10. SHROUD	J.	Voiced a shrill, broken laugh
I -	11. TRUNDLED	K.	Excessive pride in one's appearance
V -	12. FETID	L.	Taking a risk or braving dangers
U -	13. ABHORRED	M.	Tightly drawn; tense
R -	14. FORGE	N.	Obscene; vulgar; abusive
P -	15. AILS	O.	In a fatigued, tired, or worn-out way
O -	16. WEARILY	P.	Causes physical or emotional pain
Q -	17. WHARVES	Q.	Landing places where ships may tie up to load or unload
L -	18. VENTURING	R.	Workshop of a blacksmith
S -	19. VEHEMENTLY	S.	With great passion or energy
Y -	20. TRIFLING	T.	Extremely unpleasant or distasteful in regards to sickness
B -	21. DISENTANGLING	U.	Detested utterly; loathed; hated
H -	22. LOITERING	V.	Having an offensive odor
C -	23. FAMISHED	W.	Noisy commotion or disturbance
T -	24. BILIOUS	X.	Rotten; decaying
K -	25. VANITY	Y.	Small; of little importance

Fever 1793 Vocabulary Matching 3

___ 1. PLACID   A. Taking a risk or braving dangers
___ 2. IMPLORE   B. Beg urgently
___ 3. INVALID   C. Quiet; calm; peaceful
___ 4. VEHEMENTLY   D. Cleanse; purify
___ 5. HARRUMPHED   E. Voiced a shrill, broken laugh
___ 6. WEARILY   F. Persuading with flattery or promises
___ 7. TAUT   G. Extremely thin and bony
___ 8. BEGRUDGE   H. Offered brief, critical comments
___ 9. BESTIR   I. With great passion or energy
___ 10. BILIOUS   J. Moved along
___ 11. RESOLUTELY   K. Small; of little importance
___ 12. VICTUALS   L. Noisy commotion or disturbance
___ 13. DESTITUTE   M. Shake or wave a weapon
___ 14. CACKLED   N. In a fatigued, tired, or worn-out way
___ 15. TRUNDLED   O. Lacking food, clothing, and shelter; without necessities
___ 16. GUMPTION   P. Firmly determined
___ 17. CAJOLING   Q. Someone too weak to care for himself
___ 18. PURGE   R. Food fit for humans to eat
___ 19. EXTINGUISH   S. Extremely hungry
___ 20. TRIFLING   T. Extremely unpleasant or distasteful in regards to sickness
___ 21. VENTURING   U. Aggressiveness; boldness
___ 22. GAUNT   V. Put out or bring to an end
___ 23. BRANDISH   W. Stir up; rouse; bring to action
___ 24. FAMISHED   X. Tightly drawn; tense
___ 25. RUCKUS   Y. Envy or resent the good fortune of someone else

Fever 1793 Vocabulary Matching 3 Answer Key

C - 1.	PLACID	A.	Taking a risk or braving dangers
B - 2.	IMPLORE	B.	Beg urgently
Q - 3.	INVALID	C.	Quiet; calm; peaceful
I - 4.	VEHEMENTLY	D.	Cleanse; purify
H - 5.	HARRUMPHED	E.	Voiced a shrill, broken laugh
N - 6.	WEARILY	F.	Persuading with flattery or promises
X - 7.	TAUT	G.	Extremely thin and bony
Y - 8.	BEGRUDGE	H.	Offered brief, critical comments
W - 9.	BESTIR	I.	With great passion or energy
T - 10.	BILIOUS	J.	Moved along
P - 11.	RESOLUTELY	K.	Small; of little importance
R - 12.	VICTUALS	L.	Noisy commotion or disturbance
O - 13.	DESTITUTE	M.	Shake or wave a weapon
E - 14.	CACKLED	N.	In a fatigued, tired, or worn-out way
J - 15.	TRUNDLED	O.	Lacking food, clothing, and shelter; without necessities
U - 16.	GUMPTION	P.	Firmly determined
F - 17.	CAJOLING	Q.	Someone too weak to care for himself
D - 18.	PURGE	R.	Food fit for humans to eat
V - 19.	EXTINGUISH	S.	Extremely hungry
K - 20.	TRIFLING	T.	Extremely unpleasant or distasteful in regards to sickness
A - 21.	VENTURING	U.	Aggressiveness; boldness
G - 22.	GAUNT	V.	Put out or bring to an end
M - 23.	BRANDISH	W.	Stir up; rouse; bring to action
S - 24.	FAMISHED	X.	Tightly drawn; tense
L - 25.	RUCKUS	Y.	Envy or resent the good fortune of someone else

Fever 1793 Vocabulary Matching 4

___ 1. TRUNDLED	A. Poisonous fumes or germs polluting the atmosphere
___ 2. FETID	B. Quality of being offensively bold; nerve; rudeness
___ 3. BUNKUM	C. In a fatigued, tired, or worn-out way
___ 4. VICTUALS	D. Insincere or ridiculous talk
___ 5. FORGE	E. Lifted; raised up
___ 6. COMMOTION	F. Firmly determined
___ 7. HASTE	G. Tolerate; put up with; stay
___ 8. ABHORRED	H. Persuading with flattery or promises
___ 9. GAUNT	I. Tightly drawn; tense
___ 10. BESTIR	J. Serious; not to be taken lightly
___ 11. IMPUDENCE	K. Having a yellow discoloration of the skin due to disease
___ 12. JAUNDICED	L. Small; of little importance
___ 13. TAUT	M. Swiftness of motion; hurry; rush
___ 14. WEARILY	N. Weariness from bodily or mental exhaustion
___ 15. HOISTED	O. Workshop of a blacksmith
___ 16. RESOLUTELY	P. Excessive; extreme; unreasonable
___ 17. EXORBITANT	Q. Taking a risk or braving dangers
___ 18. FATIGUE	R. Disturbance; chaotic activity
___ 19. MIASMA	S. Food fit for humans to eat
___ 20. TRIFLING	T. Extremely thin and bony
___ 21. VENTURING	U. Offered brief, critical comments
___ 22. HARRUMPHED	V. Detested utterly; loathed; hated
___ 23. SOLEMN	W. Having an offensive odor
___ 24. CAJOLING	X. Moved along
___ 25. ABIDE	Y. Stir up; rouse; bring to action

Fever 1793 Vocabulary Matching 4 Answer Key

X - 1. TRUNDLED
W - 2. FETID
D - 3. BUNKUM
S - 4. VICTUALS
O - 5. FORGE
R - 6. COMMOTION
M - 7. HASTE
V - 8. ABHORRED
T - 9. GAUNT
Y - 10. BESTIR
B - 11. IMPUDENCE
K - 12. JAUNDICED
I - 13. TAUT
C - 14. WEARILY
E - 15. HOISTED
F - 16. RESOLUTELY
P - 17. EXORBITANT
N - 18. FATIGUE
A - 19. MIASMA
L - 20. TRIFLING
Q - 21. VENTURING
U - 22. HARRUMPHED
J - 23. SOLEMN
H - 24. CAJOLING
G - 25. ABIDE

A. Poisonous fumes or germs polluting the atmosphere
B. Quality of being offensively bold; nerve; rudeness
C. In a fatigued, tired, or worn-out way
D. Insincere or ridiculous talk
E. Lifted; raised up
F. Firmly determined
G. Tolerate; put up with; stay
H. Persuading with flattery or promises
I. Tightly drawn; tense
J. Serious; not to be taken lightly
K. Having a yellow discoloration of the skin due to disease
L. Small; of little importance
M. Swiftness of motion; hurry; rush
N. Weariness from bodily or mental exhaustion
O. Workshop of a blacksmith
P. Excessive; extreme; unreasonable
Q. Taking a risk or braving dangers
R. Disturbance; chaotic activity
S. Food fit for humans to eat
T. Extremely thin and bony
U. Offered brief, critical comments
V. Detested utterly; loathed; hated
W. Having an offensive odor
X. Moved along
Y. Stir up; rouse; bring to action

Fever 1793 Vocabulary Magic Squares 1

Match the definition with the vocabulary word. Put your answers in the magic squares below. When your answers are correct, all columns and rows will add to the same number.

A. SCURRILOUS
B. WHARVES
C. WEARILY
D. AILS
E. DROLL
F. HOISTED
G. FETID
H. SALVAGE
I. TRUNDLED
J. BEGRUDGE
K. DEMURE
L. GAUNT
M. PROPRIETOR
N. MIASMA
O. FAMISHED
P. EXTINGUISH

1. Poisonous fumes or germs polluting the atmosphere
2. Having an offensive odor
3. Extremely thin and bony
4. Obscene; vulgar; abusive
5. Shy; modest; coy
6. Landing places where ships may tie up to load or unload
7. Owner of a business establishment
8. Save; rescue
9. Amusing or funny in an odd or dry way
10. Put out or bring to an end
11. In a fatigued, tired, or worn-out way
12. Envy or resent the good fortune of someone else
13. Causes physical or emotional pain
14. Moved along
15. Lifted; raised up
16. Extremely hungry

A=	B=	C=	D=
E=	F=	G=	H=
I=	J=	K=	L=
M=	N=	O=	P=

Fever 1793 Vocabulary Magic Squares 1 Answer Key

Match the definition with the vocabulary word. Put your answers in the magic squares below. When your answers are correct, all columns and rows will add to the same number.

- A. SCURRILOUS
- B. WHARVES
- C. WEARILY
- D. AILS
- E. DROLL
- F. HOISTED
- G. FETID
- H. SALVAGE
- I. TRUNDLED
- J. BEGRUDGE
- K. DEMURE
- L. GAUNT
- M. PROPRIETOR
- N. MIASMA
- O. FAMISHED
- P. EXTINGUISH

1. Poisonous fumes or germs polluting the atmosphere
2. Having an offensive odor
3. Extremely thin and bony
4. Obscene; vulgar; abusive
5. Shy; modest; coy
6. Landing places where ships may tie up to load or unload
7. Owner of a business establishment
8. Save; rescue
9. Amusing or funny in an odd or dry way
10. Put out or bring to an end
11. In a fatigued, tired, or worn-out way
12. Envy or resent the good fortune of someone else
13. Causes physical or emotional pain
14. Moved along
15. Lifted; raised up
16. Extremely hungry

A=4	B=6	C=11	D=13
E=9	F=15	G=2	H=8
I=14	J=12	K=5	L=3
M=7	N=1	O=16	P=10

Fever 1793 Vocabulary Magic Squares 2

Match the definition with the vocabulary word. Put your answers in the magic squares below. When your answers are correct, all columns and rows will add to the same number.

A. TRIFLING   G. VANITY   M. BUNKUM
B. AILS   H. WEARILY   N. FATIGUE
C. GUMPTION   I. TAUT   O. TRUNDLED
D. RESOLUTELY   J. EXORBITANT   P. GAUNT
E. INVALID   K. SOLITARY
F. BEGRUDGE   L. ABIDE

1. Moved along
2. Firmly determined
3. Excessive; extreme; unreasonable
4. Someone too weak to care for himself
5. Tightly drawn; tense
6. Envy or resent the good fortune of someone else
7. Extremely thin and bony
8. Aggressiveness; boldness
9. In a fatigued, tired, or worn-out way
10. Alone or unattended
11. Small; of little importance
12. Weariness from bodily or mental exhaustion
13. Causes physical or emotional pain
14. Insincere or ridiculous talk
15. Excessive pride in one's appearance
16. Tolerate; put up with; stay

A=	B=	C=	D=
E=	F=	G=	H=
I=	J=	K=	L=
M=	N=	O=	P=

Fever 1793 Vocabulary Magic Squares 2 Answer Key

Match the definition with the vocabulary word. Put your answers in the magic squares below. When your answers are correct, all columns and rows will add to the same number.

A. TRIFLING
B. AILS
C. GUMPTION
D. RESOLUTELY
E. INVALID
F. BEGRUDGE
G. VANITY
H. WEARILY
I. TAUT
J. EXORBITANT
K. SOLITARY
L. ABIDE
M. BUNKUM
N. FATIGUE
O. TRUNDLED
P. GAUNT

1. Moved along
2. Firmly determined
3. Excessive; extreme; unreasonable
4. Someone too weak to care for himself
5. Tightly drawn; tense
6. Envy or resent the good fortune of someone else
7. Extremely thin and bony
8. Aggressiveness; boldness
9. In a fatigued, tired, or worn-out way
10. Alone or unattended
11. Small; of little importance
12. Weariness from bodily or mental exhaustion
13. Causes physical or emotional pain
14. Insincere or ridiculous talk
15. Excessive pride in one's appearance
16. Tolerate; put up with; stay

A=11	B=13	C=8	D=2
E=4	F=6	G=15	H=9
I=5	J=3	K=10	L=16
M=14	N=12	O=1	P=7

Fever 1793 Vocabulary Magic Squares 3

Match the definition with the vocabulary word. Put your answers in the magic squares below. When your answers are correct, all columns and rows will add to the same number.

A. DESTITUTE
B. GUMPTION
C. MIASMA
D. SOLEMN
E. CAJOLING
F. DIM
G. TAUT
H. TRIFLING
I. RELENT
J. CACKLED
K. SCURRILOUS
L. GAUNT
M. PLACID
N. SALVAGE
O. ABHORRED
P. CONCEDED

1. Poisonous fumes or germs polluting the atmosphere
2. Voiced a shrill, broken laugh
3. Not bright; dull
4. Detested utterly; loathed; hated
5. Yielded; admitted; relinquished; reluctantly acknowledged
6. Persuading with flattery or promises
7. Slacken; abandon; withdraw; give in
8. Serious; not to be taken lightly
9. Quiet; calm; peaceful
10. Small; of little importance
11. Extremely thin and bony
12. Lacking food, clothing, and shelter; without necessities
13. Aggressiveness; boldness
14. Obscene; vulgar; abusive
15. Tightly drawn; tense
16. Save; rescue

A=	B=	C=	D=
E=	F=	G=	H=
I=	J=	K=	L=
M=	N=	O=	P=

Fever 1793 Vocabulary Magic Squares 3 Answer Key

Match the definition with the vocabulary word. Put your answers in the magic squares below. When your answers are correct, all columns and rows will add to the same number.

A. DESTITUTE
B. GUMPTION
C. MIASMA
D. SOLEMN
E. CAJOLING
F. DIM

G. TAUT
H. TRIFLING
I. RELENT
J. CACKLED
K. SCURRILOUS
L. GAUNT

M. PLACID
N. SALVAGE
O. ABHORRED
P. CONCEDED

1. Poisonous fumes or germs polluting the atmosphere
2. Voiced a shrill, broken laugh
3. Not bright; dull
4. Detested utterly; loathed; hated
5. Yielded; admitted; relinquished; reluctantly acknowledged
6. Persuading with flattery or promises
7. Slacken; abandon; withdraw; give in
8. Serious; not to be taken lightly
9. Quiet; calm; peaceful
10. Small; of little importance
11. Extremely thin and bony
12. Lacking food, clothing, and shelter; without necessities
13. Aggressiveness; boldness
14. Obscene; vulgar; abusive
15. Tightly drawn; tense
16. Save; rescue

A=12	B=13	C=1	D=8
E=6	F=3	G=15	H=10
I=7	J=2	K=14	L=11
M=9	N=16	O=4	P=5

Fever 1793 Vocabulary Magic Squares 4

Match the definition with the vocabulary word. Put your answers in the magic squares below. When your answers are correct, all columns and rows will add to the same number.

A. WEARILY
B. LOITERING
C. DROLL
D. INVALID
E. TRIFLING
F. TRUNDLED
G. SNIPPET
H. JAUNDICED
I. FORGE
J. EXTINGUISH
K. FATIGUE
L. MELODIOUS
M. PLACID
N. ABHORRED
O. BEGRUDGE
P. PUTRID

1. Having a yellow discoloration of the skin due to disease
2. Quiet; calm; peaceful
3. Lingering aimlessly; hanging about with no purpose
4. Weariness from bodily or mental exhaustion
5. Put out or bring to an end
6. Amusing or funny in an odd or dry way
7. Rotten; decaying
8. Small; of little importance
9. Envy or resent the good fortune of someone else
10. Moved along
11. Workshop of a blacksmith
12. Someone too weak to care for himself
13. In a fatigued, tired, or worn-out way
14. Sweet-sounding
15. Small or insignificant person
16. Detested utterly; loathed; hated

A=	B=	C=	D=
E=	F=	G=	H=
I=	J=	K=	L=
M=	N=	O=	P=

Fever 1793 Vocabulary Magic Squares 4 Answer Key

Match the definition with the vocabulary word. Put your answers in the magic squares below. When your answers are correct, all columns and rows will add to the same number.

A. WEARILY
B. LOITERING
C. DROLL
D. INVALID
E. TRIFLING
F. TRUNDLED
G. SNIPPET
H. JAUNDICED
I. FORGE
J. EXTINGUISH
K. FATIGUE
L. MELODIOUS
M. PLACID
N. ABHORRED
O. BEGRUDGE
P. PUTRID

1. Having a yellow discoloration of the skin due to disease
2. Quiet; calm; peaceful
3. Lingering aimlessly; hanging about with no purpose
4. Weariness from bodily or mental exhaustion
5. Put out or bring to an end
6. Amusing or funny in an odd or dry way
7. Rotten; decaying
8. Small; of little importance
9. Envy or resent the good fortune of someone else
10. Moved along
11. Workshop of a blacksmith
12. Someone too weak to care for himself
13. In a fatigued, tired, or worn-out way
14. Sweet-sounding
15. Small or insignificant person
16. Detested utterly; loathed; hated

A=13	B=3	C=6	D=12
E=8	F=10	G=15	H=1
I=11	J=5	K=4	L=14
M=2	N=16	O=9	P=7

Fever 1793 Vocabulary Word Search 1

```
A I L S U O I L I B D T E R D A E C
B C G U M F S P W I N C M E M G X P
H T B O P N Q O L E N W S S B A O B
O Y T I N A V A L E L T A O E U R D
R L C D T D V E D E I I L L G N B W
R O A O C N R U T T M Z V U R T I D
E I C L I I P S U E T N A T U X T P
D T K E R M N T Y E T V G E D E A V
R E L M I B E S P H Z H E L G R N S
U R E X H Z T P T K P I E Y E U T S
C I D B O Q I W T I K M W R K M D G
K N S R I N M X F F L P E P E E W E
U G E V S F M E B O P L A C I D D S
S M V K T S T V U R U O R D R I H D
F T R X E I C C N G R R I O B R A T
B R A N D I S H K E G E L A O T S F
Q B H U F I M R U L E L Y U Y U T X
W W W W T D M V M Y W H D X H P E Q
```

ABHORRED	DEMURE	HASTE	MIASMA	SHROUD
ABIDE	DESTITUTE	HOISTED	PLACID	SNIPPET
AILS	DIM	IMPLORE	PURGE	SOLEMN
BEGRUDGE	DROLL	IMPUDENCE	PUTRID	TAUT
BILIOUS	EXORBITANT	INSTILL	RELENT	TETHERED
BRANDISH	FETID	INVALID	RESOLUTELY	VANITY
BUNKUM	FORGE	LOITERING	RUCKUS	WEARILY
CACKLED	GAUNT	MELODIOUS	SALVAGE	WHARVES

Fever 1793 Vocabulary Word Search 1 Answer Key

ABHORRED	DEMURE	HASTE	MIASMA	SHROUD
ABIDE	DESTITUTE	HOISTED	PLACID	SNIPPET
AILS	DIM	IMPLORE	PURGE	SOLEMN
BEGRUDGE	DROLL	IMPUDENCE	PUTRID	TAUT
BILIOUS	EXORBITANT	INSTILL	RELENT	TETHERED
BRANDISH	FETID	INVALID	RESOLUTELY	VANITY
BUNKUM	FORGE	LOITERING	RUCKUS	WEARILY
CACKLED	GAUNT	MELODIOUS	SALVAGE	WHARVES

Fever 1793 Vocabulary Word Search 2

```
S O L E M N L O I T E R I N G F D P
W E A R I L Y S R S I L B E S T I R
R E R O L P M I L U N D V B T H S O
D P E S K V C I T O S I I L E H E P
E R S C Z I A U T I T L P D T O N R
X U O D I C A L P D I A F P H I A I
T C L L D T M H S O L V A U E S A E
I K U W L U S N U L L N T T R T N T
N U T E E A A S Q E D I I R E E G O
G S E C G L I B M M E X G I D D L R
U O L N A S M R E G M M U D D E I D
I L Y E V J G W R G U L E T F R N Y
S I R L L P O O S H R O U D M R G G
H T E I A H F L H P E U E I B O Q R
A A L T S L G Z I V U D D X R H T F
S R E S F E T I D N I R T G H B L F
T Y N E G A U N T B G H G L E A W C
E P T P R C V F A M I S H E D P R F
```

ABHORRED	EXTINGUISH	LOITERING	SALVAGE
ABIDE	FAMISHED	MELODIOUS	SHROUD
AILS	FATIGUE	MIASMA	SNIPPET
BEGRUDGE	FETID	PESTILENCE	SOLEMN
BESTIR	FORGE	PLACID	SOLITARY
BILIOUS	GAUNT	PROPRIETOR	TAUT
CAJOLING	HASTE	PURGE	TETHERED
DEMURE	HOISTED	PUTRID	VICTUALS
DIM	IMPLORE	RELENT	WEARILY
DISENTANGLING	INSTILL	RESOLUTELY	
DROLL	INVALID	RUCKUS	

Fever 1793 Vocabulary Word Search 2 Answer Key

```
S O L E M N L O I T E R I N G     D   P
W E A R I L Y     S   I   B E S T I   R
    E R O L P M I   L U N D   B   H   O
D   E       V   I T O S I   I T   O   P
E   S       I   A U   I L P F H   I   R
X   U   D   C   L P   D L A U E   S   I
T   C   L   A   T M   O L N T R   T   E
I   K   U   L   U S   L E I R E   A   T
N   U   T E E A A     E D G E D   N   O
G   S   E C G L B     M   U D     G   R
U   O   L N A S M     E   E       L
I   L   Y E V J       R   E       I
S   I   R L   O O S H R O U D   M N
H   T   E A   F L P E U E I     R G
A   A   L S   I I U D D         R
S   R   T     F E T I D N I R   O
T   Y   E     G A U N T B G G E A
E       P           F A M I S H E D
```

ABHORRED	EXTINGUISH	LOITERING	SALVAGE
ABIDE	FAMISHED	MELODIOUS	SHROUD
AILS	FATIGUE	MIASMA	SNIPPET
BEGRUDGE	FETID	PESTILENCE	SOLEMN
BESTIR	FORGE	PLACID	SOLITARY
BILIOUS	GAUNT	PROPRIETOR	TAUT
CAJOLING	HASTE	PURGE	TETHERED
DEMURE	HOISTED	PUTRID	VICTUALS
DIM	IMPLORE	RELENT	WEARILY
DISENTANGLING	INSTILL	RESOLUTELY	
DROLL	INVALID	RUCKUS	

Fever 1793 Vocabulary Word Search 3

```
D C R C B T P Y Q H E D I L A V N I
E R Q C J E L R S X E X S L H E I P
M H O S D I G I O R J J M I O N M W
U N P L R T D R R P S X T T I T P V
R F P A L N B O U U R N K S S U L J
E P E U A I H Q O D O I A N T R O C
W W C R T B H I Z I G L E I E I R X
H P B A A R D Q T C V E J T D N E Y
A X N Q C O I P T A P D G H O G K W
R T M S L K M D G J X I B B R R Y R
V F Z E O U L E Y O X B C O L Z Z R
E H M V G L F E X L V A F P O R J Z
S F K P I C E F D I Y R A T I L O S
P A C B M C S M Y N D L M R T R Q G
C M B Y B N T M N G U G I E E I Y C
M I G U I Y E U T R O A A L R T H H
J S S P N T G T A X R U S E I S A F
Z H P V V K R W A L H N M N N E S Z
F E T I D R U C K U S T A T G B T D
T D D I M F P M Y K T V A I L S E C
```

Aggressiveness; boldness (8)
Alone or unattended (8)
Amusing or funny in an odd or dry way (5)
Beg urgently (7)
Causes physical or emotional pain (4)
Cleanse; purify (5)
Cloth or sheet wrapping a corpse (6)
Detested utterly; loathed; hated (8)
Envy or resent the good fortune of someone else (8)
Excessive pride in one's appearance (6)
Excessive; extreme; unreasonable (10)
Extremely hungry (8)
Extremely thin and bony (5)
Food fit for humans to eat (8)
Gradually put something into someone's mind or feelings (7)
Having an offensive odor (5)
In a fatigued, tired, or worn-out way (7)
Insincere or ridiculous talk (6)
Landing places where ships may tie up to load or unload (7)
Lifted; raised up (7)
Lingering aimlessly; hanging about with no purpose (9)
Noisy commotion or disturbance (6)
Not bright; dull (3)
Owner of a business establishment (10)
Persuading with flattery or promises (8)
Poisonous fumes or germs polluting the atmosphere (6)
Rotten; decaying (6)
Save; rescue (7)
Serious; not to be taken lightly (6)
Shake or wave a weapon (8)
Shy; modest; coy (6)
Slacken; abandon; withdraw; give in (6)
Small or insignificant person (7)
Someone too weak to care for himself (7)
Stir up; rouse; bring to action (6)
Sweet-sounding (9)
Swiftness of motion; hurry; rush (5)
Taking a risk or braving dangers (9)
Tightly drawn; tense (4)
Tolerate; put up with; stay (5)
Voiced a shrill, broken laugh (7)
Workshop of a blacksmith (5)

Fever 1793 Vocabulary Word Search 3 Answer Key

```
D           B       P   Y   H E D I L A V N I
  E   R           E L R S X E           L H E I
  M     O           I G I O R           I O N M
  U       L   R       D R R P S         T I T P
  R         P A L N B O U U R N         S U R L
  E         E U A I H   O D O I A N     T T I O
W H       W C R T B   I       G L E I   E D N R
  A         B A A R D   T C   V E       D O G E
  R           N   C   O   P   A D           R
  T           T   S L K M D G J   I         R
  V               E O U L E       B     O
  E               M V G L E       A F   L
  S   F               E D I Y R A T I L O S
      A                 C S M   N D   M R T R
      M     B           N T   N G U G I E E I Y
      I       U   I     E U     O A A L R T H
      S       P N       G T A   R U S E I S A
      H         P       K R A L H N M N N E S T
F E T I D R U C K U S T A T G B T
T D D I M     P M       T V A I L S E
```

Aggressiveness; boldness (8)
Alone or unattended (8)
Amusing or funny in an odd or dry way (5)
Beg urgently (7)
Causes physical or emotional pain (4)
Cleanse; purify (5)
Cloth or sheet wrapping a corpse (6)
Detested utterly; loathed; hated (8)
Envy or resent the good fortune of someone else (8)
Excessive pride in one's appearance (6)
Excessive; extreme; unreasonable (10)
Extremely hungry (8)
Extremely thin and bony (5)
Food fit for humans to eat (8)
Gradually put something into someone's mind or feelings (7)
Having an offensive odor (5)
In a fatigued, tired, or worn-out way (7)
Insincere or ridiculous talk (6)
Landing places where ships may tie up to load or unload (7)
Lifted; raised up (7)
Lingering aimlessly; hanging about with no purpose (9)
Noisy commotion or disturbance (6)
Not bright; dull (3)
Owner of a business establishment (10)
Persuading with flattery or promises (8)
Poisonous fumes or germs polluting the atmosphere (6)
Rotten; decaying (6)
Save; rescue (7)
Serious; not to be taken lightly (6)
Shake or wave a weapon (8)
Shy; modest; coy (6)
Slacken; abandon; withdraw; give in (6)
Small or insignificant person (7)
Someone too weak to care for himself (7)
Stir up; rouse; bring to action (6)
Sweet-sounding (9)
Swiftness of motion; hurry; rush (5)
Taking a risk or braving dangers (9)
Tightly drawn; tense (4)
Tolerate; put up with; stay (5)
Voiced a shrill, broken laugh (7)
Workshop of a blacksmith (5)

Fever 1793 Vocabulary Word Search 4

```
P T R I F L I N G A U N T C N N V K
U E Z E G D U R G E B R D M O V I R
T C S Y G S Y U P T X I E I W A C B
R A Y T N P R C L B T L T N X N T Z
I C G B I S F K N E O P I S L I U X
D K S I R L D U F S M S M T M T A C
L L P L E X E S F U J N P I W Y L P
R E D I T V D N G F A I L L H Q S F
C D S O I E E F C M U P O L G Y B K
B D O U O M T Y Z E N P R N L E J V
X D L S L A S H R G D E E I S T D X
W Y I C M Q I F E W I T R T W F T P
E H T S N S O N T R C A I R B W U F
R H A S T E H P D D E R R O H B A C
U I R R S S L R U W D D E A Z M T Z
M A Y N V A K S O R S F B L I K J T
E I P C C E G R O U G I O S E W Y S
D L X I B C S L Q P D E H R H N L H
I S D J F T L D V E J E M S G N T J
M U K N U B M E L O D I O U S E D P
```

A deadly disease (10)
Aggressiveness; boldness (8)
Alone or unattended (8)
Amusing or funny in an odd or dry way (5)
Attached by a short rope (8)
Beg urgently (7)
Causes physical or emotional pain (4)
Cleanse; purify (5)
Cloth or sheet wrapping a corpse (6)
Detested utterly; loathed; hated (8)
Envy or resent the good fortune of someone else (8)
Excessive pride in one's appearance (6)
Extremely hungry (8)
Extremely thin and bony (5)
Extremely unpleasant or distasteful in regards to sickness (7)
Food fit for humans to eat (8)
Gradually put something into someone's mind or feelings (7)
Having a yellow discoloration of the skin due to disease (9)
Having an offensive odor (5)
In a fatigued, tired, or worn-out way (7)

Insincere or ridiculous talk (6)
Landing places where ships may tie up to load or unload (7)
Lifted; raised up (7)
Lingering aimlessly; hanging about with no purpose (9)
Noisy commotion or disturbance (6)
Not bright; dull (3)
Poisonous fumes or germs polluting the atmosphere (6)
Quiet; calm; peaceful (6)
Rotten; decaying (6)
Serious; not to be taken lightly (6)
Shy; modest; coy (6)
Slacken; abandon; withdraw; give in (6)
Small or insignificant person (7)
Small; of little importance (8)
Stir up; rouse; bring to action (6)
Sweet-sounding (9)
Swiftness of motion; hurry; rush (5)
Tightly drawn; tense (4)
Tolerate; put up with; stay (5)
Voiced a shrill, broken laugh (7)
Workshop of a blacksmith (5)

Fever 1793 Vocabulary Word Search 4 Answer Key

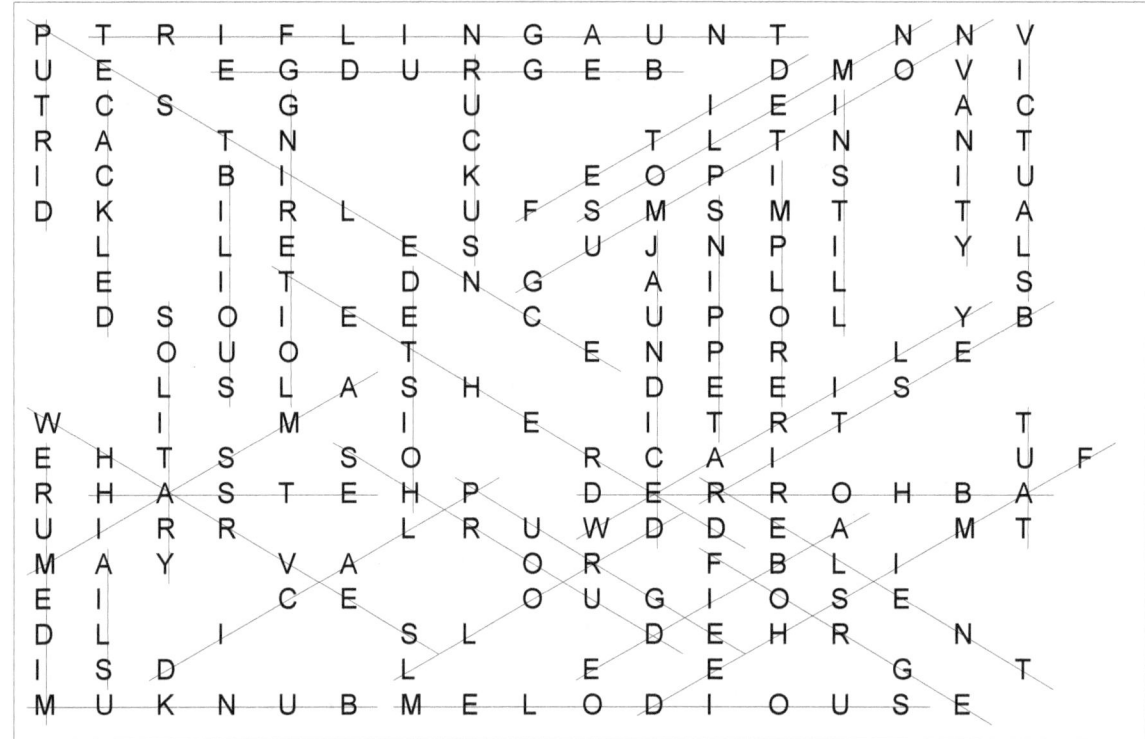

A deadly disease (10)
Aggressiveness; boldness (8)
Alone or unattended (8)
Amusing or funny in an odd or dry way (5)
Attached by a short rope (8)
Beg urgently (7)
Causes physical or emotional pain (4)
Cleanse; purify (5)
Cloth or sheet wrapping a corpse (6)
Detested utterly; loathed; hated (8)
Envy or resent the good fortune of someone else (8)
Excessive pride in one's appearance (6)
Extremely hungry (8)
Extremely thin and bony (5)
Extremely unpleasant or distasteful in regards to sickness (7)
Food fit for humans to eat (8)
Gradually put something into someone's mind or feelings (7)
Having a yellow discoloration of the skin due to disease (9)
Having an offensive odor (5)
In a fatigued, tired, or worn-out way (7)

Insincere or ridiculous talk (6)
Landing places where ships may tie up to load or unload (7)
Lifted; raised up (7)
Lingering aimlessly; hanging about with no purpose (9)
Noisy commotion or disturbance (6)
Not bright; dull (3)
Poisonous fumes or germs polluting the atmosphere (6)
Quiet; calm; peaceful (6)
Rotten; decaying (6)
Serious; not to be taken lightly (6)
Shy; modest; coy (6)
Slacken; abandon; withdraw; give in (6)
Small or insignificant person (7)
Small; of little importance (8)
Stir up; rouse; bring to action (6)
Sweet-sounding (9)
Swiftness of motion; hurry; rush (5)
Tightly drawn; tense (4)
Tolerate; put up with; stay (5)
Voiced a shrill, broken laugh (7)
Workshop of a blacksmith (5)

Fever 1793 Vocabulary Crossword 1

Across
1. Disturbance; chaotic activity
2. Swiftness of motion; hurry; rush
4. Excessive pride in one's appearance
7. Extremely thin and bony
9. Offered brief, critical comments
12. Not bright; dull
13. Lifted; raised up
15. Envy or resent the good fortune of someone else
17. Amusing or funny in an odd or dry way
19. Noisy commotion or disturbance
20. Cloth or sheet wrapping a corpse
21. Stir up; rouse; bring to action
22. Yielded; admitted; relinquished; reluctantly acknowledged

Down
1. Voiced a shrill, broken laugh
3. Moved along
4. With great passion or energy
5. Tightly drawn; tense
6. Attached by a short rope
8. Causes physical or emotional pain
10. Slacken; abandon; withdraw; give in
11. Cleanse; purify
14. Tolerate; put up with; stay
15. Insincere or ridiculous talk
16. Shy; modest; coy
18. Rotten; decaying

Fever 1793 Vocabulary Crossword 1 Answer Key

Across
1. Disturbance; chaotic activity
2. Swiftness of motion; hurry; rush
4. Excessive pride in one's appearance
7. Extremely thin and bony
9. Offered brief, critical comments
12. Not bright; dull
13. Lifted; raised up
15. Envy or resent the good fortune of someone else
17. Amusing or funny in an odd or dry way
19. Noisy commotion or disturbance
20. Cloth or sheet wrapping a corpse
21. Stir up; rouse; bring to action
22. Yielded; admitted; relinquished; reluctantly acknowledged

Down
1. Voiced a shrill, broken laugh
3. Moved along
4. With great passion or energy
5. Tightly drawn; tense
6. Attached by a short rope
8. Causes physical or emotional pain
10. Slacken; abandon; withdraw; give in
11. Cleanse; purify
14. Tolerate; put up with; stay
15. Insincere or ridiculous talk
16. Shy; modest; coy
18. Rotten; decaying

Fever 1793 Vocabulary Crossword 2

Across
1. Offered brief, critical comments
4. Landing places where ships may tie up to load or unload
7. Envy or resent the good fortune of someone else
10. Poisonous fumes or germs polluting the atmosphere
12. Shy; modest; coy
16. Causes physical or emotional pain
17. Not bright; dull
19. Lingering aimlessly; hanging about with no purpose
21. Extremely thin and bony
22. Noisy commotion or disturbance

Down
1. Lifted; raised up
2. Slacken; abandon; withdraw; give in
3. Cleanse; purify
5. With great passion or energy
6. Rotten; decaying
7. Insincere or ridiculous talk
8. Aggressiveness; boldness
9. Voiced a shrill, broken laugh
11. Sweet-sounding
12. Amusing or funny in an odd or dry way
13. Weariness from bodily or mental exhaustion
14. Beg urgently
15. Workshop of a blacksmith
18. Having an offensive odor
20. Tightly drawn; tense

Fever 1793 Vocabulary Crossword 2 Answer Key

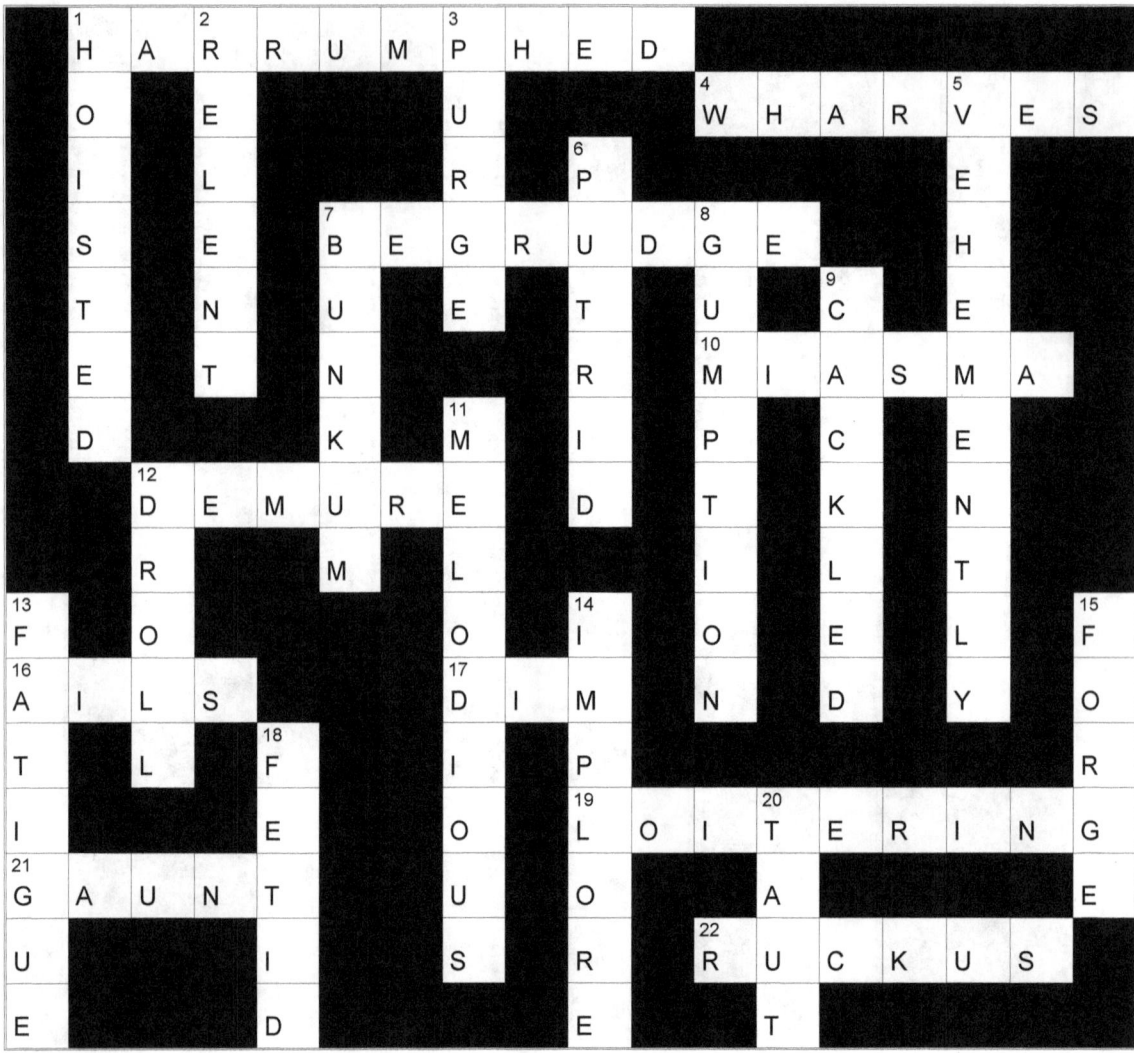

Across
1. Offered brief, critical comments
4. Landing places where ships may tie up to load or unload
7. Envy or resent the good fortune of someone else
10. Poisonous fumes or germs polluting the atmosphere
12. Shy; modest; coy
16. Causes physical or emotional pain
17. Not bright; dull
19. Lingering aimlessly; hanging about with no purpose
21. Extremely thin and bony
22. Noisy commotion or disturbance

Down
1. Lifted; raised up
2. Slacken; abandon; withdraw; give in
3. Cleanse; purify
5. With great passion or energy
6. Rotten; decaying
7. Insincere or ridiculous talk
8. Aggressiveness; boldness
9. Voiced a shrill, broken laugh
11. Sweet-sounding
12. Amusing or funny in an odd or dry way
13. Weariness from bodily or mental exhaustion
14. Beg urgently
15. Workshop of a blacksmith
18. Having an offensive odor
20. Tightly drawn; tense

Fever 1793 Vocabulary Crossword 3

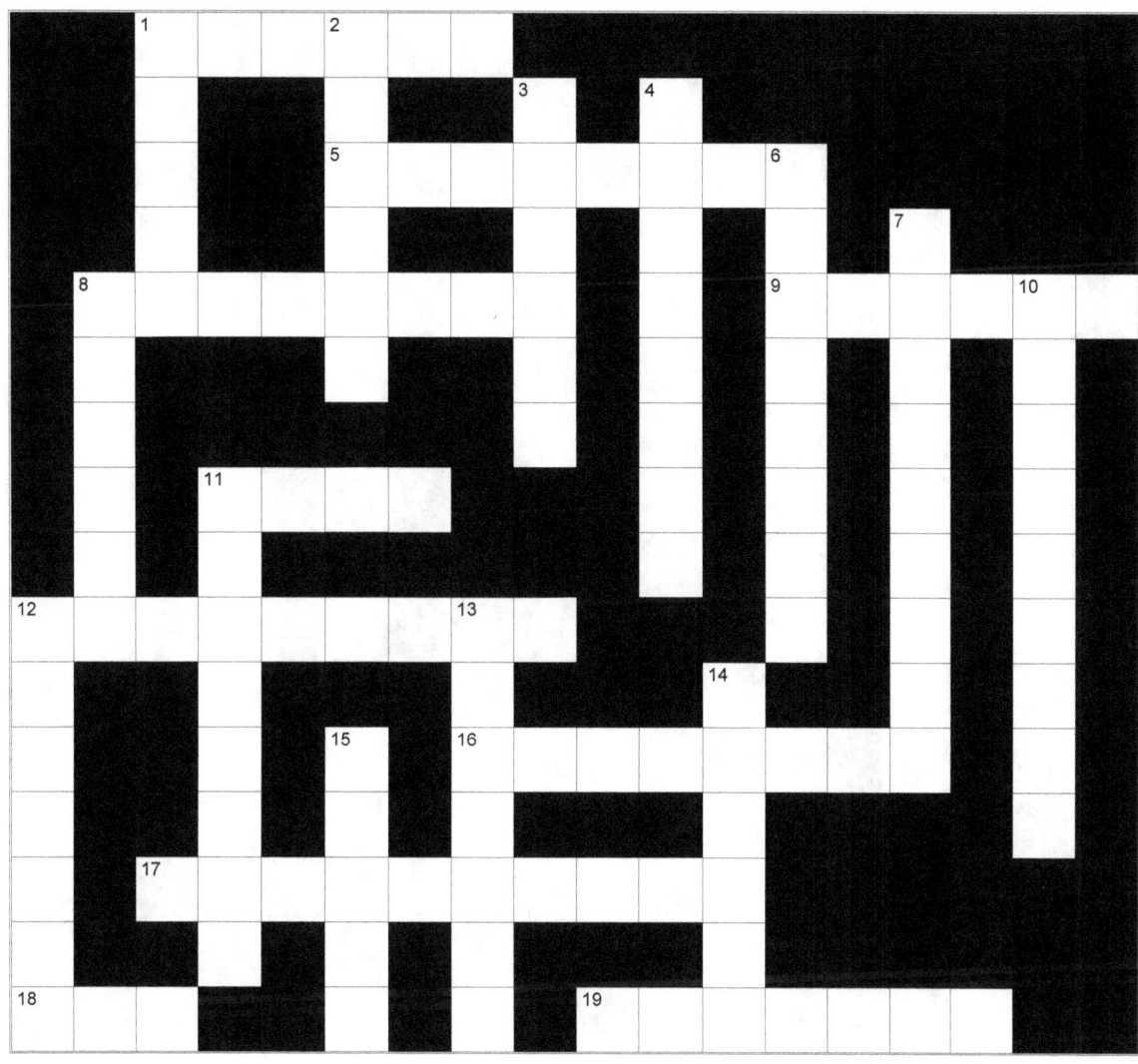

Across
1. Rotten; decaying
5. Persuading with flattery or promises
8. Envy or resent the good fortune of someone else
9. Poisonous fumes or germs polluting the atmosphere
11. Tightly drawn; tense
12. Quality of being offensively bold; nerve; rudeness
16. Yielded; admitted; relinquished; reluctantly acknowledged
17. A deadly disease
18. Not bright; dull
19. Weariness from bodily or mental exhaustion

Down
1. Cleanse; purify
2. Noisy commotion or disturbance
3. Serious; not to be taken lightly
4. Food fit for humans to eat
6. Aggressiveness; boldness
7. Having a yellow discoloration of the skin due to disease
8. Insincere or ridiculous talk
10. Sweet-sounding
11. Moved along
12. Someone too weak to care for himself
13. Voiced a shrill, broken laugh
14. Slacken; abandon; withdraw; give in
15. Having an offensive odor

Fever 1793 Vocabulary Crossword 3 Answer Key

Across
1. Rotten; decaying
5. Persuading with flattery or promises
8. Envy or resent the good fortune of someone else
9. Poisonous fumes or germs polluting the atmosphere
11. Tightly drawn; tense
12. Quality of being offensively bold; nerve; rudeness
16. Yielded; admitted; relinquished; reluctantly acknowledged
17. A deadly disease
18. Not bright; dull
19. Weariness from bodily or mental exhaustion

Down
1. Cleanse; purify
2. Noisy commotion or disturbance
3. Serious; not to be taken lightly
4. Food fit for humans to eat
6. Aggressiveness; boldness
7. Having a yellow discoloration of the skin due to disease
8. Insincere or ridiculous talk
10. Sweet-sounding
11. Moved along
12. Someone too weak to care for himself
13. Voiced a shrill, broken laugh
14. Slacken; abandon; withdraw; give in
15. Having an offensive odor

Fever 1793 Vocabulary Crossword 4

Across
1. Alone or unattended
6. Voiced a shrill, broken laugh
8. Small or insignificant person
10. Extremely thin and bony
12. Causes physical or emotional pain
13. Gradually put something into someone's mind or feelings
15. Workshop of a blacksmith
17. Stir up; rouse; bring to action
19. Swiftness of motion; hurry; rush
20. Extremely hungry
21. Owner of a business establishment
22. Beg urgently
23. Aggressiveness; boldness

Down
1. Serious; not to be taken lightly
2. Tightly drawn; tense
3. Noisy commotion or disturbance
4. Extremely unpleasant or distasteful in regards to sickness
5. Obscene; vulgar; abusive
7. Shy; modest; coy
8. Save; rescue
9. Quiet; calm; peaceful
11. Attached by a short rope
14. Lingering aimlessly; hanging about with no purpose
16. Not bright; dull
18. Rotten; decaying
20. Having an offensive odor

Fever 1793 Crossword 4 Answer Key

Across
1. Alone or unattended
6. Voiced a shrill, broken laugh
8. Small or insignificant person
10. Extremely thin and bony
12. Causes physical or emotional pain
13. Gradually put something into someone's mind or feelings
15. Workshop of a blacksmith
17. Stir up; rouse; bring to action
19. Swiftness of motion; hurry; rush
20. Extremely hungry
21. Owner of a business establishment
22. Beg urgently
23. Aggressiveness; boldness

Down
1. Serious; not to be taken lightly
2. Tightly drawn; tense
3. Noisy commotion or disturbance
4. Extremely unpleasant or distasteful in regards to sickness
5. Obscene; vulgar; abusive
7. Shy; modest; coy
8. Save; rescue
9. Quiet; calm; peaceful
11. Attached by a short rope
14. Lingering aimlessly; hanging about with no purpose
16. Not bright; dull
18. Rotten; decaying
20. Having an offensive odor

Fever 1793 Vocabulary Juggle Letters 1

1. RTPRPOEOIR = 1. _____
   Owner of a business establishment

2. RILEWYA = 2. _____
   In a fatigued, tired, or worn-out way

3. TNPPSIE = 3. _____
   Small or insignificant person

4. EPCNLIETES = 4. _____
   A deadly disease

5. IUMPGTON = 5. _____
   Aggressiveness; boldness

6. LNLISIT = 6. _____
   Gradually put something into someone's mind or feelings

7. UKBNMU = 7. _____
   Insincere or ridiculous talk

8. CACLKED = 8. _____
   Voiced a shrill, broken laugh

9. ADLICP = 9. _____
   Quiet; calm; peaceful

10. SAAMMI = 10. _____
    Poisonous fumes or germs polluting the atmosphere

11. RODHEABR = 11. _____
    Detested utterly; loathed; hated

12. RGEUP = 12. _____
    Cleanse; purify

13. LIOGJCAN = 13. _____
    Persuading with flattery or promises

14. TRTDEHEE = 14. _____
    Attached by a short rope

Fever 1793 Vocabulary Juggle Letters 1 Answer Key

1. RTPRPOEOIR = 1. PROPRIETOR
   Owner of a business establishment

2. RILEWYA = 2. WEARILY
   In a fatigued, tired, or worn-out way

3. TNPPSIE = 3. SNIPPET
   Small or insignificant person

4. EPCNLIETES = 4. PESTILENCE
   A deadly disease

5. IUMPGTON = 5. GUMPTION
   Aggressiveness; boldness

6. LNLISIT = 6. INSTILL
   Gradually put something into someone's mind or feelings

7. UKBNMU = 7. BUNKUM
   Insincere or ridiculous talk

8. CACLKED = 8. CACKLED
   Voiced a shrill, broken laugh

9. ADLICP = 9. PLACID
   Quiet; calm; peaceful

10. SAAMMI =10. MIASMA
    Poisonous fumes or germs polluting the atmosphere

11. RODHEABR =11. ABHORRED
    Detested utterly; loathed; hated

12. RGEUP =12. PURGE
    Cleanse; purify

13. LIOGJCAN =13. CAJOLING
    Persuading with flattery or promises

14. TRTDEHEE =14. TETHERED
    Attached by a short rope

Fever 1793 Vocabulary Juggle Letters 2

1. RLLDO = 1. _____
   Amusing or funny in an odd or dry way

2. TSCLEIEENP = 2. _____
   A deadly disease

3. AUIFTEG = 3. _____
   Weariness from bodily or mental exhaustion

4. ONDEDCEC = 4. _____
   Yielded; admitted; relinquished; reluctantly acknowledged

5. IFRNTILG = 5. _____
   Small; of little importance

6. NTEGVRINU = 6. _____
   Taking a risk or braving dangers

7. LOUIBSI = 7. _____
   Extremely unpleasant or distasteful in regards to sickness

8. ATUT = 8. _____
   Tightly drawn; tense

9. IWRLEAY = 9. _____
   In a fatigued, tired, or worn-out way

10. BEOTAITNXR =10. _____
    Excessive; extreme; unreasonable

11. IBDAE =11. _____
    Tolerate; put up with; stay

12. NMDEEICPU =12. _____
    Quality of being offensively bold; nerve; rudeness

13. RITBSE =13. _____
    Stir up; rouse; bring to action

14. DENTULRD =14. _____
    Moved along

Fever 1793 Vocabulary Juggle Letters 2 Answer Key

1. RLLDO = 1. DROLL
Amusing or funny in an odd or dry way

2. TSCLEIEENP = 2. PESTILENCE
A deadly disease

3. AUIFTEG = 3. FATIGUE
Weariness from bodily or mental exhaustion

4. ONDEDCEC = 4. CONCEDED
Yielded; admitted; relinquished; reluctantly acknowledged

5. IFRNTILG = 5. TRIFLING
Small; of little importance

6. NTEGVRINU = 6. VENTURING
Taking a risk or braving dangers

7. LOUIBSI = 7. BILIOUS
Extremely unpleasant or distasteful in regards to sickness

8. ATUT = 8. TAUT
Tightly drawn; tense

9. IWRLEAY = 9. WEARILY
In a fatigued, tired, or worn-out way

10. BEOTAITNXR = 10. EXORBITANT
Excessive; extreme; unreasonable

11. IBDAE = 11. ABIDE
Tolerate; put up with; stay

12. NMDEEICPU = 12. IMPUDENCE
Quality of being offensively bold; nerve; rudeness

13. RITBSE = 13. BESTIR
Stir up; rouse; bring to action

14. DENTULRD = 14. TRUNDLED
Moved along

Fever 1793 Vocabulary Juggle Letters 3

1. RAHBDSNI = 1. _____
   Shake or wave a weapon

2. RTUIPD = 2. _____
   Rotten; decaying

3. SETLOUERYL = 3. _____
   Firmly determined

4. DRHSUO = 4. _____
   Cloth or sheet wrapping a corpse

5. DEANIJCUD = 5. _____
   Having a yellow discoloration of the skin due to disease

6. LSIA = 6. _____
   Causes physical or emotional pain

7. ELWAYIR = 7. _____
   In a fatigued, tired, or worn-out way

8. GNNERVIUT = 8. _____
   Taking a risk or braving dangers

9. SURSROCILU = 9. _____
   Obscene; vulgar; abusive

10. TGNUA = 10. _____
    Extremely thin and bony

11. OTMOCNIOM = 11. _____
    Disturbance; chaotic activity

12. LDTEDUNR = 12. _____
    Moved along

13. SUCIAVLT = 13. _____
    Food fit for humans to eat

14. DMERUE = 14. _____
    Shy; modest; coy

Fever 1793 Vocabulary Juggle Letters 3 Answer Key

1. RAHBDSNI = 1. BRANDISH
   Shake or wave a weapon

2. RTUIPD = 2. PUTRID
   Rotten; decaying

3. SETLOUERYL = 3. RESOLUTELY
   Firmly determined

4. DRHSUO = 4. SHROUD
   Cloth or sheet wrapping a corpse

5. DEANIJCUD = 5. JAUNDICED
   Having a yellow discoloration of the skin due to disease

6. LSIA = 6. AILS
   Causes physical or emotional pain

7. ELWAYIR = 7. WEARILY
   In a fatigued, tired, or worn-out way

8. GNNERVIUT = 8. VENTURING
   Taking a risk or braving dangers

9. SURSROCILU = 9. SCURRILOUS
   Obscene; vulgar; abusive

10. TGNUA =10. GAUNT
    Extremely thin and bony

11. OTMOCNIOM =11. COMMOTION
    Disturbance; chaotic activity

12. LDTEDUNR =12. TRUNDLED
    Moved along

13. SUCIAVLT =13. VICTUALS
    Food fit for humans to eat

14. DMERUE =14. DEMURE
    Shy; modest; coy

Fever 1793 Vocabulary Juggle Letters 4

1. EMRDUE = 1. _____
   Shy; modest; coy

2. HSIIENTGUX = 2. _____
   Put out or bring to an end

3. MID = 3. _____
   Not bright; dull

4. TIORGEILN = 4. _____
   Lingering aimlessly; hanging about with no purpose

5. NAVLDII = 5. _____
   Someone too weak to care for himself

6. MUUBNK = 6. _____
   Insincere or ridiculous talk

7. ILMEUSOOD = 7. _____
   Sweet-sounding

8. XBRTITANOE = 8. _____
   Excessive; extreme; unreasonable

9. AIPDLC = 9. _____
   Quiet; calm; peaceful

10. OSILURUSCR = 10. _____
    Obscene; vulgar; abusive

11. HOBRREAD = 11. _____
    Detested utterly; loathed; hated

12. OIPREML = 12. _____
    Beg urgently

13. IBAHDRNS = 13. _____
    Shake or wave a weapon

14. AEASLGV = 14. _____
    Save; rescue

Fever 1793 Vocabulary Juggle Letters 4 Answer Key

1. EMRDUE = 1. DEMURE
Shy; modest; coy

2. HSIIENTGUX = 2. EXTINGUISH
Put out or bring to an end

3. MID = 3. DIM
Not bright; dull

4. TIORGEILN = 4. LOITERING
Lingering aimlessly; hanging about with no purpose

5. NAVLDII = 5. INVALID
Someone too weak to care for himself

6. MUUBNK = 6. BUNKUM
Insincere or ridiculous talk

7. ILMEUSOOD = 7. MELODIOUS
Sweet-sounding

8. XBRTITANOE = 8. EXORBITANT
Excessive; extreme; unreasonable

9. AIPDLC = 9. PLACID
Quiet; calm; peaceful

10. OSILURUSCR =10. SCURRILOUS
Obscene; vulgar; abusive

11. HOBRREAD =11. ABHORRED
Detested utterly; loathed; hated

12. OIPREML =12. IMPLORE
Beg urgently

13. IBAHDRNS =13. BRANDISH
Shake or wave a weapon

14. AEASLGV =14. SALVAGE
Save; rescue

ABHORRED	Detested utterly; loathed; hated
ABIDE	Tolerate; put up with; stay
AILS	Causes physical or emotional pain
BEGRUDGE	Envy or resent the good fortune of someone else
BESTIR	Stir up; rouse; bring to action

BILIOUS	Extremely unpleasant or distasteful in regards to sickness
BRANDISH	Shake or wave a weapon
BUNKUM	Insincere or ridiculous talk
CACKLED	Voiced a shrill, broken laugh
CAJOLING	Persuading with flattery or promises

COMMOTION	Disturbance; chaotic activity
CONCEDED	Yielded; admitted; relinquished; reluctantly acknowledged
DEMURE	Shy; modest; coy
DESTITUTE	Lacking food, clothing, and shelter; without necessities
DIM	Not bright; dull

DISENTANGLING	Unravelling; becoming free from
DROLL	Amusing or funny in an odd or dry way
EXORBITANT	Excessive; extreme; unreasonable
EXTINGUISH	Put out or bring to an end
FAMISHED	Extremely hungry

FATIGUE	Weariness from bodily or mental exhaustion
FETID	Having an offensive odor
FORGE	Workshop of a blacksmith
GAUNT	Extremely thin and bony
GUMPTION	Aggressiveness; boldness

HARRUMPHED	Offered brief, critical comments
HASTE	Swiftness of motion; hurry; rush
HOISTED	Lifted; raised up
IMPLORE	Beg urgently
IMPUDENCE	Quality of being offensively bold; nerve; rudeness

INSTILL	Gradually put something into someone's mind or feelings
INVALID	Someone too weak to care for himself
JAUNDICED	Having a yellow discoloration of the skin due to disease
LOITERING	Lingering aimlessly; hanging about with no purpose
MELODIOUS	Sweet-sounding

MIASMA	Poisonous fumes or germs polluting the atmosphere
PESTILENCE	A deadly disease
PLACID	Quiet; calm; peaceful
PROPRIETOR	Owner of a business establishment
PURGE	Cleanse; purify

PUTRID	Rotten; decaying
RELENT	Slacken; abandon; withdraw; give in
RESOLUTELY	Firmly determined
RUCKUS	Noisy commotion or disturbance
SALVAGE	Save; rescue

SCURRILOUS	Obscene; vulgar; abusive
SHROUD	Cloth or sheet wrapping a corpse
SNIPPET	Small or insignificant person
SOLEMN	Serious; not to be taken lightly
SOLITARY	Alone or unattended

TAUT	Tightly drawn; tense
TETHERED	Attached by a short rope
TRIFLING	Small; of little importance
TRUNDLED	Moved along
VANITY	Excessive pride in one's appearance

VEHEMENTLY	With great passion or energy
VENTURING	Taking a risk or braving dangers
VICTUALS	Food fit for humans to eat
WEARILY	In a fatigued, tired, or worn-out way
WHARVES	Landing places where ships may tie up to load or unload

Fever 1793 Vocabulary

TAUT	HASTE	INVALID	CONCEDED	IMPLORE
SALVAGE	DESTITUTE	DEMURE	TRIFLING	WEARILY
INSTILL	RELENT	FREE SPACE	PURGE	EXTINGUISH
DROLL	BILIOUS	SOLEMN	EXORBITANT	AILS
COMMOTION	ABIDE	FORGE	RUCKUS	SCURRILOUS

Fever 1793 Vocabulary

SNIPPET	CAJOLING	RESOLUTELY	VENTURING	FATIGUE
IMPUDENCE	LOITERING	VANITY	GUMPTION	GAUNT
TETHERED	BEGRUDGE	FREE SPACE	PROPRIETOR	ABHORRED
VEHEMENTLY	BUNKUM	FAMISHED	PUTRID	SOLITARY
FETID	HARRUMPHED	DIM	PESTILENCE	HOISTED

Fever 1793 Vocabulary

GUMPTION	TRIFLING	SOLITARY	TETHERED	SOLEMN
BILIOUS	GAUNT	VANITY	PURGE	INSTILL
RESOLUTELY	VENTURING	FREE SPACE	DESTITUTE	HARRUMPHED
CONCEDED	RELENT	AILS	ABHORRED	LOITERING
DIM	HASTE	WHARVES	SCURRILOUS	RUCKUS

Fever 1793 Vocabulary

DROLL	EXTINGUISH	FATIGUE	VICTUALS	PLACID
BUNKUM	PUTRID	FAMISHED	COMMOTION	PROPRIETOR
MELODIOUS	MIASMA	FREE SPACE	BEGRUDGE	DEMURE
IMPUDENCE	PESTILENCE	HOISTED	FORGE	TRUNDLED
CAJOLING	BESTIR	EXORBITANT	ABIDE	JAUNDICED

Fever 1793 Vocabulary

DEMURE	TETHERED	HASTE	SCURRILOUS	IMPLORE
DESTITUTE	IMPUDENCE	FETID	JAUNDICED	ABIDE
BESTIR	FORGE	FREE SPACE	PLACID	MIASMA
LOITERING	GAUNT	SNIPPET	EXORBITANT	VENTURING
RUCKUS	DISENTANGLING	WEARILY	TAUT	GUMPTION

Fever 1793 Vocabulary

BEGRUDGE	RESOLUTELY	VANITY	ABHORRED	BRANDISH
SOLITARY	CONCEDED	PROPRIETOR	PESTILENCE	DROLL
EXTINGUISH	VICTUALS	FREE SPACE	PURGE	SOLEMN
MELODIOUS	HOISTED	TRIFLING	WHARVES	COMMOTION
HARRUMPHED	DIM	RELENT	INVALID	FATIGUE

Fever 1793 Vocabulary

ABIDE	PUTRID	MIASMA	DIM	JAUNDICED
SOLEMN	WHARVES	SALVAGE	CAJOLING	VICTUALS
TRUNDLED	VANITY	FREE SPACE	SCURRILOUS	LOITERING
CONCEDED	RELENT	BEGRUDGE	HOISTED	VENTURING
GAUNT	PROPRIETOR	BUNKUM	DESTITUTE	FETID

Fever 1793 Vocabulary

FATIGUE	WEARILY	INVALID	SHROUD	EXTINGUISH
IMPLORE	IMPUDENCE	VEHEMENTLY	TAUT	DROLL
DISENTANGLING	CACKLED	FREE SPACE	FORGE	FAMISHED
GUMPTION	TRIFLING	EXORBITANT	RESOLUTELY	BRANDISH
PURGE	SNIPPET	PESTILENCE	DEMURE	COMMOTION

Fever 1793 Vocabulary

MIASMA	TAUT	EXORBITANT	SALVAGE	ABIDE
DEMURE	RELENT	DIM	EXTINGUISH	SOLEMN
CONCEDED	PURGE	FREE SPACE	BRANDISH	BESTIR
PUTRID	TRUNDLED	GUMPTION	BILIOUS	IMPLORE
FATIGUE	RESOLUTELY	DISENTANGLING	TRIFLING	HARRUMPHED

Fever 1793 Vocabulary

TETHERED	VENTURING	LOITERING	PESTILENCE	DESTITUTE
FETID	DROLL	PLACID	RUCKUS	HASTE
VANITY	PROPRIETOR	FREE SPACE	SHROUD	CACKLED
VICTUALS	FORGE	ABHORRED	SNIPPET	VEHEMENTLY
IMPUDENCE	GAUNT	AILS	JAUNDICED	BEGRUDGE

Fever 1793 Vocabulary

BRANDISH	HOISTED	DROLL	CACKLED	EXORBITANT
TRIFLING	HARRUMPHED	SOLITARY	RELENT	WEARILY
RESOLUTELY	INVALID	FREE SPACE	PURGE	ABHORRED
LOITERING	FORGE	IMPLORE	SOLEMN	SALVAGE
TETHERED	CAJOLING	VENTURING	FATIGUE	BEGRUDGE

Fever 1793 Vocabulary

HASTE	BESTIR	MIASMA	DISENTANGLING	MELODIOUS
FAMISHED	GUMPTION	PROPRIETOR	BILIOUS	SHROUD
COMMOTION	PUTRID	FREE SPACE	AILS	SCURRILOUS
RUCKUS	PESTILENCE	GAUNT	VICTUALS	DEMURE
TAUT	SNIPPET	VEHEMENTLY	IMPUDENCE	DESTITUTE

Fever 1793 Vocabulary

DISENTANGLING	PESTILENCE	BILIOUS	RESOLUTELY	TAUT
WEARILY	EXORBITANT	BRANDISH	INVALID	MIASMA
BESTIR	COMMOTION	FREE SPACE	GUMPTION	DROLL
SOLEMN	EXTINGUISH	VEHEMENTLY	INSTILL	IMPUDENCE
SHROUD	PUTRID	HARRUMPHED	TRUNDLED	PROPRIETOR

Fever 1793 Vocabulary

ABIDE	WHARVES	TRIFLING	HASTE	JAUNDICED
CACKLED	RELENT	GAUNT	VANITY	FATIGUE
FORGE	DEMURE	FREE SPACE	BUNKUM	BEGRUDGE
IMPLORE	DESTITUTE	HOISTED	DIM	CAJOLING
PLACID	FAMISHED	TETHERED	AILS	VICTUALS

Fever 1793 Vocabulary

HOISTED	IMPUDENCE	PLACID	CONCEDED	HASTE
RUCKUS	PROPRIETOR	MIASMA	PESTILENCE	INSTILL
SHROUD	BESTIR	FREE SPACE	VENTURING	HARRUMPHED
AILS	RESOLUTELY	TRUNDLED	EXTINGUISH	WEARILY
TAUT	DEMURE	ABIDE	DISENTANGLING	EXORBITANT

Fever 1793 Vocabulary

BUNKUM	DESTITUTE	DROLL	FETID	FAMISHED
VEHEMENTLY	BEGRUDGE	SALVAGE	SOLITARY	SOLEMN
COMMOTION	SNIPPET	FREE SPACE	ABHORRED	DIM
TRIFLING	WHARVES	CAJOLING	INVALID	VICTUALS
BILIOUS	FORGE	RELENT	PUTRID	GAUNT

Fever 1793 Vocabulary

PLACID	DISENTANGLING	ABHORRED	INVALID	DIM
BEGRUDGE	TRUNDLED	COMMOTION	INSTILL	HASTE
GUMPTION	TETHERED	FREE SPACE	MIASMA	TRIFLING
WHARVES	EXORBITANT	EXTINGUISH	GAUNT	BESTIR
FETID	CONCEDED	FAMISHED	PURGE	PUTRID

Fever 1793 Vocabulary

SNIPPET	SOLITARY	RUCKUS	SOLEMN	FATIGUE
RESOLUTELY	HOISTED	BUNKUM	AILS	WEARILY
DEMURE	SALVAGE	FREE SPACE	PESTILENCE	VEHEMENTLY
CAJOLING	VANITY	HARRUMPHED	DROLL	SHROUD
IMPUDENCE	DESTITUTE	RELENT	CACKLED	MELODIOUS

Fever 1793 Vocabulary

HARRUMPHED	TRIFLING	EXORBITANT	DEMURE	INVALID
FATIGUE	GAUNT	LOITERING	SHROUD	MELODIOUS
TAUT	PURGE	FREE SPACE	INSTILL	EXTINGUISH
BUNKUM	VEHEMENTLY	CACKLED	PESTILENCE	CONCEDED
DIM	CAJOLING	SCURRILOUS	ABHORRED	DISENTANGLING

Fever 1793 Vocabulary

VENTURING	WEARILY	GUMPTION	TRUNDLED	PUTRID
JAUNDICED	DESTITUTE	VANITY	SOLITARY	TETHERED
FAMISHED	DROLL	FREE SPACE	ABIDE	PLACID
IMPUDENCE	RESOLUTELY	IMPLORE	COMMOTION	HASTE
BEGRUDGE	RUCKUS	RELENT	SNIPPET	BILIOUS

Fever 1793 Vocabulary

TRUNDLED	PLACID	PROPRIETOR	TETHERED	EXORBITANT
SHROUD	HOISTED	BESTIR	FETID	AILS
MIASMA	RUCKUS	FREE SPACE	LOITERING	PUTRID
DESTITUTE	RESOLUTELY	FATIGUE	CAJOLING	RELENT
ABIDE	DEMURE	INVALID	JAUNDICED	EXTINGUISH

Fever 1793 Vocabulary

TAUT	PURGE	BEGRUDGE	SNIPPET	GAUNT
ABHORRED	IMPUDENCE	CONCEDED	BILIOUS	WHARVES
TRIFLING	FORGE	FREE SPACE	SOLEMN	DIM
FAMISHED	VEHEMENTLY	DISENTANGLING	IMPLORE	SCURRILOUS
WEARILY	BUNKUM	VANITY	INSTILL	HARRUMPHED

Fever 1793 Vocabulary

RELENT	MIASMA	SOLEMN	INSTILL	WEARILY
TAUT	HASTE	BESTIR	FORGE	BEGRUDGE
BUNKUM	FETID	FREE SPACE	EXORBITANT	RUCKUS
VEHEMENTLY	BRANDISH	FATIGUE	RESOLUTELY	DROLL
SALVAGE	SCURRILOUS	PLACID	TRUNDLED	MELODIOUS

Fever 1793 Vocabulary

SNIPPET	VENTURING	SOLITARY	AILS	EXTINGUISH
COMMOTION	VICTUALS	TETHERED	SHROUD	GAUNT
HARRUMPHED	DESTITUTE	FREE SPACE	PESTILENCE	DISENTANGLING
HOISTED	INVALID	CAJOLING	FAMISHED	BILIOUS
TRIFLING	CACKLED	IMPUDENCE	ABHORRED	IMPLORE

Fever 1793 Vocabulary

RESOLUTELY	HOISTED	RELENT	VANITY	DROLL
BEGRUDGE	GUMPTION	MELODIOUS	PUTRID	PROPRIETOR
SOLEMN	INVALID	FREE SPACE	LOITERING	EXTINGUISH
BESTIR	COMMOTION	BRANDISH	SALVAGE	HASTE
EXORBITANT	SOLITARY	DESTITUTE	WEARILY	SHROUD

Fever 1793 Vocabulary

HARRUMPHED	VEHEMENTLY	GAUNT	VENTURING	IMPUDENCE
FORGE	SCURRILOUS	VICTUALS	FATIGUE	TRIFLING
TAUT	DIM	FREE SPACE	WHARVES	MIASMA
ABIDE	BILIOUS	DISENTANGLING	SNIPPET	IMPLORE
BUNKUM	FAMISHED	AILS	PESTILENCE	FETID

Fever 1793 Vocabulary

SCURRILOUS	CONCEDED	DIM	EXTINGUISH	BRANDISH
PURGE	GAUNT	JAUNDICED	MIASMA	BEGRUDGE
FETID	RUCKUS	FREE SPACE	FORGE	PUTRID
WEARILY	SOLITARY	CACKLED	ABIDE	GUMPTION
CAJOLING	AILS	SHROUD	BILIOUS	TETHERED

Fever 1793 Vocabulary

HASTE	RELENT	DESTITUTE	DISENTANGLING	TAUT
ABHORRED	EXORBITANT	SNIPPET	SALVAGE	BESTIR
VANITY	DROLL	FREE SPACE	FAMISHED	VENTURING
RESOLUTELY	IMPUDENCE	VEHEMENTLY	VICTUALS	PESTILENCE
TRIFLING	INVALID	HOISTED	PLACID	INSTILL

Fever 1793 Vocabulary

CONCEDED	JAUNDICED	IMPUDENCE	TRIFLING	BILIOUS
GUMPTION	DIM	VICTUALS	PROPRIETOR	HARRUMPHED
ABIDE	TETHERED	FREE SPACE	EXTINGUISH	RELENT
COMMOTION	INSTILL	CACKLED	AILS	DISENTANGLING
INVALID	CAJOLING	BESTIR	BUNKUM	SCURRILOUS

Fever 1793 Vocabulary

PLACID	RUCKUS	IMPLORE	WHARVES	HASTE
VEHEMENTLY	LOITERING	FATIGUE	SNIPPET	BEGRUDGE
MELODIOUS	MIASMA	FREE SPACE	VANITY	TAUT
WEARILY	RESOLUTELY	BRANDISH	FAMISHED	FORGE
PUTRID	DROLL	PESTILENCE	SOLEMN	SOLITARY

Fever 1793 Vocabulary

INSTILL	COMMOTION	RUCKUS	VICTUALS	BILIOUS
SCURRILOUS	TRIFLING	PUTRID	GUMPTION	JAUNDICED
VANITY	RESOLUTELY	FREE SPACE	CONCEDED	CAJOLING
PLACID	IMPLORE	BEGRUDGE	BUNKUM	DESTITUTE
DIM	ABIDE	VEHEMENTLY	TAUT	SNIPPET

Fever 1793 Vocabulary

WEARILY	PURGE	TETHERED	GAUNT	SOLEMN
INVALID	BRANDISH	IMPUDENCE	DISENTANGLING	BESTIR
PROPRIETOR	DROLL	FREE SPACE	RELENT	DEMURE
SALVAGE	HARRUMPHED	HASTE	TRUNDLED	ABHORRED
EXORBITANT	LOITERING	MIASMA	AILS	PESTILENCE